WWII Pilot, Betrayal, Then Congressional Gold Medal

A Great Ride for WASP, Jean Landis

Sonya Nesch

White Trillium Press
P.O. Box 309, Comptche, CA 95427
707-937-3339

WWII Pilot, Betrayal, Then Congressional Gold Medal: A Great Ride for WASP, Jean Landis

White Trillium Press
P.O. Box 309
Comptche, CA 95427
707-939-3339
www.whitetrilliumpress.com

Ordering Information:

Special discounts are available on quantity purchases. For details, contact White Trillium Press at the address above.

Library of Congress Cataloging-in-Publication Data
Nesch, Sonya
WWII Pilot, Betrayal, Then Congressional Gold Medal: A Great Ride for WASP, Jean Landis/Sonya Nesch - 1st ed.

p. cm.

ISBN 978-0-9755565-1-1

Subjects: 1. WASP. 2. Biography. 3. Women Pilots 4. WWII

CONTENTS

ACKNOWLEDGEMENTS

I am grateful above all to Jean Landis as this book could not have been written without the substantial amount of time she put into it. She told me stories, shared the WASP information she had saved, answered all my questions, and read the manuscript multiple times.

The Award Winning DVD about Jean Landis, *She Wore Silver Wings* by American Dream Cinema, was enormously helpful and provided important inspiration for me. It was written and directed by Jean's grand nephew, Devin Scott, and produced by his wife, Jeanne Scott.

My heartfelt thanks to Karen Lewis for an early read that provided valuable direction for me, to Jan Boyd for copyediting, and to Doug Fortier for getting me across the finish line.

My deep gratitude goes to the people who have memorialized the WASP in print and on the Internet. Because of them, all of us can now learn much more about the lives of the amazing women of WASP.

The first women to fly United States military planes were the WASP, Women Airforce Service Pilots. During the initial 18 months of WWII, 1,074 female pilots flew 60 million miles in 77 types of aircraft, and on every kind of mission except combat. They were stationed at more than 50 of the 120 Army Air Force Bases across America.

This book is the WASP experience seen through the memories of my cousin, Jean Landis, with some historical context. I have included a few profiles of other WASP that Jean knew, to expand understanding of the women that were the first to fly military airplanes in the face of strong cultural and gender bias against women in nontraditional roles. These well-qualified and heroic women served our country and developed some long-lasting relationships with their sisters in WASP. They were extraordinary women: independent, adventurous, intelligent, talented, strong-minded, and willing to step up to important and risky work to serve America in a time of war.

The betrayal by the United States government in denying the promised militarization of WASP, and the sealing of their military records for 33 years, excluded them from a place in U.S. history books.

In contrast with the WACs and WAVEs, they received no military benefits and had to pass the hat to send the bodies and belongings of WASP who died in service to our country, home to their families. WASP received lesser pay than their military counterparts with no promotion or advancement possible. They had no health insurance or death insurance, and no access to the GI Bill for Education or Veteran Home Loan Program. In addition, they suffered the sabotage of planes they flew, and the organized opposition of men up to the highest levels of government.

WASP services were finally acknowledged 33 years later in 1977, and the betrayal by Congress corrected, although in a half-hearted way. Women were finally granted military status and could fly military aircraft again. Further honor came in 2010 when President Barack Obama awarded the well-deserved Congressional Gold Medal to the WASP, 66 years after their WWII service. By 2016, women could serve in all military combat roles and be buried at Arlington National Cemetery.

1: Letter to Senator Barry Goldwater from Jean Landis in 1977

Jean Landis wrote a good synopsis of the WASP journey in her letter to Senator Barry Goldwater, published in *The Stars and Stripes—The National Tribune* on October 6, 1977.

"One Of The First, Still Forced To Be Last"
September 22, 1977

The Honorable Barry Goldwater
United States Senate
Washington, D.C. 20510

Dear Sir:

Thank you so very much for your heroic efforts in behalf of the WASPs.

To add a little fuel to your fire, I will relate my sad story.

In 1940, having just graduated from college at age 21, I accepted a teaching job at a local high school.

Approximately two years later, Pearl Harbor was bombed. I was an experienced pilot and eager to serve my country. When the "call" came out that there was a need for women with flying experience to deliver planes and release some of our men for more hazardous missions, I was one of the first to volunteer. I was assured that soon we would be militarized. Therefore, I left my teaching position ON A MILITARY LEAVE OF ABSENCE.

After flying almost every type of aircraft built, from fighters to four engine, in almost every kind of weather imaginable, and after

1

"seeing" 38 of my colleagues killed in line of duty, and after taking up collections to send their clothes home, and after paying my own dentist bills and appendectomy bills while serving my country, and after receiving less pay than many men who had less experience and training than I, and upon our deactivation, I found I had lost my job! Why? Because I had not been militarized. I had no GI Bill of Rights, no insurance, no hospitalization... nothing! I worked my way through graduate school at Wellesley College while all of my classmates who were WACs and WAVEs paid nothing.

Now, approximately 34 years later when I am about to retire from the teaching profession, I find I am again being cheated out of those two years. They will not count them toward my retirement. They are simply lost. They do not count towards militarization, they do not count towards retirement, they do not count at all.

To me they were the most worthy, fulfilling and dedicated two years of my entire life. I would do it all again, even knowing as I do now, that they may never be appreciated nor acknowledged by my Country nor my fellow man. This I regret, very deeply.

I thank you for your untiring efforts.

Respectfully,
/s/ Jean Landis, WASP
12530 Royal Road, Sp.21
El Cajon, Calif. 92021

2: Jean's Family Life in El Cajon, California

Jean's parents, Felix Landis and Alice Katherine Nesch Landis, were schoolmates in Pittsburg, Kansas and became engaged when she was 15 and he was 18. They married a couple of years later in 1910. Alice had fallen in love with San Diego on a family visit, so Felix traded an old automobile for a down payment on five acres of land in El Cajon, California where they would farm and raise chickens. For five years they lived in a 14' x 20' canvas tent house they bought from the nearby Hotel del Coronado. The Hotel had a "Tent City" from the early 1900s until 1939 with reasonable rates for America's new middle class. Jean says, "The tent houses were used mostly as week-end rentals. Families with kids loved them. They were just plopped down on the sand with no floors, kids covered with sand running in and out. Who needs wood planks for flooring?"

Jean says, "My parents slept on the floor of the tent on oat hay and cooked camp style. They had 200 Leghorn hens that took shelter at night under the tent house. Dad worked for the neighbors for the first three years for 20 cents an hour, $1.80 for a 9-hour day. He plowed, cultivated, picked oranges, peaches and grapes, cut and stacked hay, worked on wells, just about anything people wanted help with. They eventually built a house for $1000 that still stands over one hundred years later," and is less than a mile from Jean's home in the Granite Hills section of El Cajon.

Jean was born in that house on September 28, 1918, the middle child of three. Felix, Jr. was two years older and Jerry was ten years younger. When Felix, Jr. and Jean were old enough, they were responsible for the irrigation system that watered the orange and avocado trees.

Felix, Jr. had a paper route and delivered papers up and down the hills of El Cajon on a small mare named Apache Maid that their father bought for $20 and a bale of hay. Jean's brother trained the horse quickly because she was smart, aware and very alert. When Felix entered high school in the ninth grade and started playing sports, Jean was in seventh grade and took over his paper route. Jean loved Apache Maid, talked to her, gave her fresh water and hay every day. Jean says, "You never knew when something would excite her and off she'd go." She loved riding Apache bareback through the neighboring orchards after chores, and even during hard rains.

Felix admired athletes and pressed his son to excel in high school sports and he did, earning eleven letters in baseball, football and track. Not to be outdone and wanting Dad's interest and approval, Jean excelled at every sport girls were allowed to play – track and field, basketball, softball, and volleyball; but they were not allowed to compete with other schools. Jean received a special award for athletics and later returned to her high school to teach all of these sports along with some tennis. Jean also excelled at academics.

Jean says, "As far back as I can remember I always wanted to learn to fly. We would only have an occasional plane overhead." Charles Lindbergh's plane for his May 21, 1927 solo transatlantic flight was built in San Diego that year. Jean was 8, and this was a big topic of conversation at home as the family followed his adventure from New York to Paris. When Jean was 13, her interest in flying was

4

sparked further by Amelia Earhart's solo nonstop flight across the Atlantic in 1932. Earhart disappeared in July 1937 during an attempt to make a circumnavigational flight around the world. Jean was 18, had been following the world flight, and remembers exactly where she was when the news broke. During summer vacations, she taught children to swim at the Hotel del Coronado. Her Dad drove her to San Diego each day to catch the Ferry. Jean's boss bought a *San Diego Union* newspaper that morning and on the front page was the heartbreaking news that Amelia Earhart had disappeared. Jean remembers how upset she was and the hard time she had focusing on teaching her students that day.

Jean was a free spirit with loving and supportive parents. They passed on no limiting beliefs about what girls should or should not do. Jean and her brothers were taught to always do their best. Her father Felix managed the San Diego County Dairymen's League and helped organize that group in 1931. He also managed the San Diego County Fair and was President of the County Farm Bureau. Felix ran unsuccessfully for San Diego County Supervisor in 1928. During the War, her mother, Alice, joined the County Farm Bureau's "Farm Home Department" where women learned about food conservation. Her father was on the Draft Board and brother Felix was drafted. He remained in San Diego at the Navy base as a Drill Sergeant. Jean remembers being "at a football game in San Diego when Pearl Harbor was hit. An announcement came over the loud speaker 'All military personnel report to your bases immediately.' We were all in shock. Later that afternoon, we got word that Pearl Harbor had been bombed."

Jean speaks lovingly of her parents. She says, "My mother was sweet and fearless. Everyone loved her and she stood up to anyone. Mom was Dad's life. After breakfast, he would often say 'That was so good honey.'" Jean wrote this tribute to her mother in 2014.

> A Tribute to the loveliest Woman I've had the privilege of knowing and loving, My Mom
>
> My Mom had an arsenal of weapons which she used to attack, treat and cure the most ferocious of maladies that threatened her brood of children. As I recall she had only five magic weapons:
>
> 1. Vick's VapoRub: Used to cure everything from a slight cold to pneumonia.
>
> 2. Campho-Phenique: Brought instant relief when used on bee stings, small cuts and abrasions.
>
> 3. Resinal: The most healing salve and soothing ointment ever invented.
>
> 4. Iodine: (The dreaded iodine) However, it kept infection at bay 100% of the time.
>
> 5. Love: The most powerful ingredient in my Mom's entire arsenal was the unending gentle love with which her healing was administered – always a soft kiss on the forehead, a sweet endearing smile, and a pat on the cheek.

No wonder I have survived for 96 years.

A tribute from your loving daughter Jean.

Today November 4, 2014 was your birthday 124 years ago!

Jean's father wrote this poem when she was 6 and visiting family in Kansas with Mom and brothers. She says, "This poem entitled 'Yearnings' may tell us more about my Dad than many thousands of words. He was, in my opinion a blend of sentimentality and harshness. I admired his honesty, his values, his ethics and the example he set for his children. (I like to think that some of it rubbed off onto me.)"

Sunday January 10, 1925 Sundown
To my Pettie.
"a little thought"

Yearnings

When evening comes and I'm alone,
In an empty house that is otherwise home,
I think the loneliest man is me.

When Sunday comes and you're away
And I miss the sounds of the children's play
The hours drag slow, it saddens me.

But the time that I miss you most of all,
Is the hour that twilight casts its pall
And the sun goes down at sea.

Dad

In 1965 when Jean was teaching at Ball State University in Muncie, Indiana, her mother died at 74 and her dad died three years later. Felix wrote to Jean "with teardrops falling on the letters as he poured his heart out. His love for Mom was unbelievable."

Felix's father was a Kansas rancher who became Warden of Kansas State Penitentiary at Lansing. Felix became interested in the violin when he heard a convict play. His father gave him a violin and the convict gave him lessons. When Jean's father retired, he was given a set of woodworking tools and began making violins in his workshop. He made five and nearly completed a sixth before his last illness. He was sick for the three years after his wife died.

3: First Flight, Teaching, and Pilot Training

On graduation night at El Cajon's Grossmont High School in 1936, Jean's date said, "What would you like most of all as a graduation present?" She knew exactly, 'I would love to take a flight in a small plane over San Diego.' Harry Garfield took us both up for a half-hour ride out of El Cajon's Gillespie Field. I knew for sure I wanted to learn to fly. I'll never forget this first spectacular flight and my dream of flying intensified."

That fall, Jean entered San Diego State Teachers College and became the first in her family to attend college. She was elected Vice President of the Associated Students in 1939, and the football team chose her for Homecoming Queen. In June 1940, Jean graduated with a B.A. degree in Physical Education. At the graduation ceremony rehearsal, they announced the newly created Civilian Pilot Training Program (CPTP) for the first 20 people who signed up at the Dean's Office. After rehearsal ended, Jean ran out the back door of the Women's Gym holding her cap to her head while her long black graduation gown flapped. She took a short cut down a dirt ravine, jumped over cactus, brush and rocks, and ran up the other side to be first to sign up at the Dean's Office. Her heart was thumping and it seemed unbelievable that her longtime dream of learning to fly planes might be possible.

The CPTP offered free pilot training to college graduates who met their requirements. Jean passed the military physical exam, was accepted and joined three other women and 16 men in the first San Diego CPTP class. She had to do some careful scheduling since she had also accepted a teaching position at her alma mater Grossmont High School.

The first CPTP class consisted of 35 hours of flight time and Jean earned a private Pilot's License in 1941. The second class required 35 hours of Aerobatics in the little Ryan Student Trainer that included: spins, dives, chandelles (180 degree turn with a climb) and Immelmann's (half loop, 180 degree roll to bring aircraft back level). In the third class of 35 hours she learned how to teach others to fly. Jean put 105 flight hours in her logbook.

CPTP was President Franklin D. Roosevelt's plan to increase the number of civilian pilots who might be available for national defense if needed. The program began in 1939 and was phased out in 1944 having trained 435,165 people to fly. There was a national quota system for women with only one woman allowed in training for every ten men. The CPTP trained around 2,500 women by mid-1941. In June 1941, one year after Jean was accepted into training, women were banned from participating in the CPTP as students; however they could be teachers. All men signed a pledge to volunteer for the Army Air Force in the event of war, but women were not allowed to fly in combat. These free classes offered a path upwards for hundreds of women and Negro pilots, even though the U.S. military was still racially segregated.

The famous Tuskegee Airmen emerged from this training and were instrumental in the eventual integration of the U.S. military in 1948. It took over three decades, for women pilots to be integrated into the Air Force in 1977. In addition to many of the WASP, other notable CPTP graduates were

Astronaut/Senator John Glenn, Senator George McGovern, Tuskegee Airman Major Robert W. Deiz.

Piloting airplanes in the late 1930's and 40's was an unusual choice for a girl or young woman. Jean says, "My parents were supportive, encouraging and behind me in every way. They never interfered with anything I wanted to do as long as it met their three conditions. It had to be of value, could not interfere with anyone else, and I had to fully commit to complete the endeavor. They never tried to discourage me from becoming a pilot." There was no parental pressure to marry and have children, or to become a secretary, nurse or teacher. Jean valued personal and economic independence, adventure, and she wanted to be a pilot.

4: Army Air Corps Says "No" then "Yes" to Female Pilots

1940 Proposals for Female Aviation Units

In the early 1940s, prior to U.S. entry into WWII, two visionary women aviators with similar dreams proposed independently to the U.S. Army Air Corps (AAC) that women could fly military planes on non-combat missions to release male pilots for combat. They were both highly intelligent and capable women with the ability to successfully implement a Female Aviation Unit.

Nancy Harkness Love (Appendix A) wrote to Lieutenant Colonel Robert Olds of the AAC Ferrying Command in May 1940, soon after WWII broke out in Europe, that she had found 49 excellent women pilots, who each had more than a thousand flying hours. They could transport planes from factories to Ferrying Command Bases. Lt. Col. Olds took the suggestion to Chief of AAC General Henry Harley "Hap" Arnold, who turned it down.

In early 1941, Jacqueline "Jackie" Cochran (Appendix B) tried to interest General Arnold in training women pilots to fly military aircraft in the U.S. and he turned her down, just as he had turned Nancy Love down the previous year. Cochran thought qualified women pilots could do all of the domestic noncombat aviation jobs and release male pilots for combat.

In March 1942, Jacqueline Cochran recruited 25 American women pilots to fly with the British Air Transport Auxiliary (ATA) under an 18-month contract. The ATA was a civilian service that delivered aircraft from factories to squadrons of the

Royal Air Force (RAF) and Royal Navy. (Appendix C)

Nancy Harkness Love and Jacqueline Cochran were very different women, one with a background of privilege and the other of poverty.

Nancy Love was well educated, a highly respected natural leader, and seemed to seep easily into the hearts of everyone who knew her.

Jackie Cochran was more distant, fiercely competitive, set seemingly impossible goals for herself and achieved most of them. You had to stand back and marvel as she reached each one with few setbacks. Her second husband is reported as saying, "Jackie has reinvented herself many times." During her lifetime, Cochran created and ran a successful cosmetics business, raced planes, joined the British Air Transport Auxiliary, created and ran an Army Air Corps training program for women pilots, and in 1956 ran unsuccessfully for Congress in California.

However, she never achieved the one goal that mattered most, Commander of the Women's Air Force. Cochran angered many female pilots when she wrote WASP history without saying much about the role their beloved Nancy Love played as Women's Auxiliary Ferrying (WAF) Squadron Commander and Executive of the Air Transport Command (ATC) Ferrying Division.

Jean says, "Jackie Cochran in her zeal to be first in everything had passionately seen to it that Nancy Harkness Love and her WAFs have been all but erased from the written history of women pilots of WWII."

4: Army Air Corps Says "No" then "Yes" to Female Pilots

Jackie Cochran wrote her autobiography with Maryann B. Brinley (Bantam Books) with the telling name *The Autobiography of the Greatest Woman Pilot in Aviation History*, published posthumously in 1987 and renamed *Jackie Cochran: An Autobiography*.

Pearl Harbor Attacked and Female Pilots are Recruited

The Japanese attacked the U.S. fleet at Pearl Harbor in Oahu just before 8 a.m. on December 7, 1941. The attack by 353 Japanese planes crippled the U.S. Pacific Fleet, and killed 2,403 Americans, wounded 1,179 others, sank or damaged 19 vessels and 188 military planes. The next day President Franklin Delano Roosevelt declared war on Japan. Four days after the Japanese attack, Germany declared war on the U.S.

The U.S. needed fighter planes and bombers with pilots to fly them. General Arnold changed his mind and asked Nancy Harkness Love to find 25 experienced women pilots to ferry military planes to various AAF Bases to release male pilots for the fighting front.

Nine months after Pearl Harbor, on September 5, 1942, General Arnold announced that women would fly military aircraft for the first time in U.S. history. He authorized the formation of the Women's Auxiliary Ferrying Squadron (WAFS) with the support of the U.S. Air Transport Command (ATC), under the command of Nancy Harkness Love. Love sent telegrams to 83 of America's best women pilots, recruiting them to deliver planes from the factory to military bases. The women must: have at least 500 hours flight time, instrument rating, Commercial Pilot License with at least a 200 horsepower rating, be no more than 35 years old, and pass a rigorous physical exam. Love found 30 qualified women who reported to her on September 21, 1942 at New Castle Army Air Base in Wilmington, Delaware. Two women were released, leaving 28 original WAFS.

Upon hearing about the formation of the WAFS, Jacqueline Cochran returned to the U.S. from England on September 8 to lobby General Arnold for a training program to expand flying opportunities beyond ferrying for women pilots.

General Arnold announced on September 15, 1942, that Cochran would lead a second women's program called Women's Flying Training Detachment (WFTD) to provide AAF Cadet Training to women. Initially 500 pilots would be trained, and later that was increased to more than 1,000 pilots.

The women must be: high school graduates or equivalent, 21 to 35 years old, and have 200 hours flying time. Upon graduation the women would be assigned to one of the four ATC bases to ferry planes under Squadron Commander Nancy Love.

There was an enormous response with 25,000 women applying for military pilot training in the WFTD. They accepted 1,830 women and Jean Landis was one of the 1,074 to successfully complete the AAF training.

4: Army Air Corps Says "No" then "Yes" to Female Pilots

The first WFTD class began November 16, 1942 at Ellington Army Air Field near Houston, Texas. The four ATC bases were located at: New Castle Army Air Field in Wilmington, Delaware; Romulus Army Air Field in Detroit, Michigan; Love Field in Dallas, Texas; and Daugherty Field in Long Beach, California.

The bases were all near aircraft manufacturing plants and the pilots were expected to deliver these planes as fast as they could to the point of embarkation, return to base, and deliver the next plane.

Jacqueline Cochran wrote to First Lady Eleanor Roosevelt in the Fall of 1940, to suggest the establishment of a Women's Flying Division of the Army Air Corps. Two years later on September 1, 1942, Roosevelt wrote the following in her "My Day" newspaper column.

> I have a letter from a gentleman who is very much exercised because our women pilots are not being utilized in the war effort. The CAA (Civil Aeronautics Administration) says that women are psychologically not fitted to be pilots, but I see pictures every now and then of women who are teaching men to fly. We know that in England where the need is great, women are ferrying planes and freeing innumerable men for combat service.
>
> It seems to me that in the civil air patrol and in our own ferry command women, if they can pass the tests imposed upon our men, should have an equal opportunity for

noncombat service.

I believe in this case, if the war goes on long enough and women are patient, opportunities will come knocking at their doors. However, there is just a chance that this is not a time when women should be patient. We are in a war and we need to fight it with all our ability and every weapon possible. Women pilots, in this particular case, are a weapon waiting to be used. As my correspondent says:

"I think it is time you women spoke up for yourselves and undertook a campaign to see that 3500 women fliers, every one of whom is anxious to do something in the war, be given a chance to do it."

Hence I am speaking up for the women fliers, because I am afraid we cannot afford to let the time slip by just now without using them.

Jean heard about the opportunity for women to take military pilot training in September 1942 while teaching Physical Education at Grossmont High School in El Cajon. She applied, passed the rigorous physical exam and met all other requirements to be accepted into the fourth class, known as 43-4. The three previous classes trained 145 women, and she would be one of 151 women in the fourth class. Her acceptance letter from the AAF Flying Training Command dated January 17, 1943 (Appendix D) said to report at her own expense to Houston, Texas and to allow "for possible delays as transportation difficulties will not be accepted as an excuse for late arrival." She would be paid $150/month and upon satisfactory completion of the Army instruction course, would be employed as a Utility Pilot and receive $250/month. Her annual salary started at $1,800 and would increase to $3,000. The average annual wage that year was $2,000. The letter also said "No provision is made for your subsistence and maintenance during the term of this appointment. No uniform will be issued during the period of the training course." A month later she received "Changes in Civilian Personnel" notice from the War Department, AAF At Large stating salary and position. (Appendix E)

Jean took a "Military Leave of Absence" from her teaching job, packed her Chevrolet Coupe with clothes, a little red desk lamp from her Aunt Lu, and set out for Ellington Army Air Field, in Houston, Texas. She had a 22 revolver hidden under the driver's seat. The five-month training program began March 15, 1943 and since she was under orders of the AAF, gas rationing was no problem. The only set back was a flat tire at night while crossing the desert. Jean says,

> They didn't have adequate barracks or equipment, and there was no mess hall. We stayed in several Auto Courts that were taken over as Barracks substitutes. I was in a small trailer bedroom with two others, there was a bathroom next to it, and a trailer bedroom with three more women next to that. There was never enough hot water. When our rooms were inspected, the inspectors wore white gloves and our sheets had to be so tight that a dime bounced off them. We got up at dark, got onto a flat bed truck by 5 a.m. and headed to PT (Physical Training) where we did jumping jacks, pushups, and other calisthenics. After breakfast we went to ground school classes: Navigation, Meteorology, Radio and Morse Code, Use of Firearms, Military Courtesy and Discipline, Military Law and Instrument Training. Then we flew for half the day. We were flying planes at 1,000 feet in open cockpits in freezing weather and without a radio. (1)

Jean remembers sitting in the cockpit blindfolded while the instructor barked, "Where's the altimeter? Where's the gas gauge? Where's the manual brake?"

Jean says, "Night flying was the most difficult. You can mistake a star for a light on a plane. With no radio contact, you relied on a map and chart, observation of ground, and visual ground checkpoints called dead reckoning." In navigation, dead reckoning (also ded for deduced reckoning or

DR) is the process of calculating one's current position by using a previously determined position or fix, and advancing that position based upon known or estimated speeds over elapsed time and course. You find one position and then looked for the next. She says,

> I never got lost or had to land at the wrong place. Many times during training for emergency   landings, my instructor chopped the throttle and my heart sunk. We were often tested by the dreaded Check Ride. A special test pilot, not your instructor, took you up to test your ability to   handle any situations he put you in. He could 'freeze' on the controls or put you in a spin and yell, 'It's all yours'. Or even worse, cut the throttle and yell 'forced landing'. You better take over immediately, head for a desirable looking landing field or something level, head into the wind, lower the landing gear, down with the flaps, and establish a normal glide. The test pilot would then take over the controls. If you failed your Check Ride the first time, you were scheduled for a second, several weeks later. If you failed the second one, you had one more chance. If you failed the third one, you packed your bags and went home. (1)

Two months after Jean started training, a base for teaching Canadian male cadets at Avenger Field in Sweetwater, Texas was made available for the WFTD. Jean and 18 other women drove their cars the 400 miles while the rest of their classmates flew BT-13s to Sweetwater to complete the training. Jean says, "The training was good and the instructors were excellent." The barracks had

21

six women to a bay, three metal cots across from each other with dark brown Army blankets, and six wooden desks in the center of the room, three across and back to back. In between our beds was a 6' x 3' metal closet. We were warned about rattlesnakes but rarely saw them as they don't want to be around people."

The training was in three phases: Primary; Basic with more instruments; and Advanced (with more horsepower, retractable gear, and even more instruments). At Avenger there were 200 airplanes – PT-17s, PT-19s, BT-13s, BT-15s, AT-6s, AT-17s, UC-78s, UC-43s and UC-81s. There were 100 "emergency" landings the first week, as male pilots wanted to get a look at the female trainees. Jackie Cochran closed the base except to real emergencies, and it got dubbed "Cochran's Convent".

At Sweetwater in the Summer of 1943, there was negative gossip in town about girl pilots running rampant. Jackie Cochran organized Vesper Services at Avenger, with different local pastors each Sunday. She also arranged meeting and social time with people in town. They were invited to the next graduation and the relationship improved.

Jean was elected Squadron Leader at Avenger Field. They marched everywhere and sang in cadence songs such as: "Stars and Stripes Forever", "This is the Army Mr. Jones", "Yankee Doodle Dandy", "You're in the Army Now", "Roll Me Over in the Clover" and "When Johnny Comes Marching Home" (Glenn Miller's 1942 hit).

Jean says, "We weren't supposed to fraternize with

the male instructors, but of course people did. There was little time for fun or socializing, as this was five months of hard work. We spent little time off base with only an occasional visit to town to grab a bite to eat. In the free time we had, we talked, played cards and sang songs while I or someone else played the ukulele. We had a ritual that everyone got dunked into the Avenger Field Wishing Well to celebrate a successful solo flight."

Creation of the WASP

Colonel Oveta Culp Hobby was Director of the Women's Army Auxiliary Corps (WAAC), later renamed the Women's Army Corps (WAC). They were created to fill gaps left by a shortage of men in: communications, rifle repair, motor pool drivers, laboratory technicians, translators, and cryptographers. WAACs were the first women, other than nurses, to be in Army uniform. Culp Hobby was the first woman in the Army to receive the Distinguished Service Medal for her efforts during the war.

Jackie Cochran and Colonel Culp Hobby met in June 1943 to talk about the women pilots military inclusion into WAAC. They had differences of opinion about who would be in charge. Cochran wanted a women's pilot organization whose members could only be assigned to flight duties. Another problem was that WAACs had to be at least 21 with no children. Some of Cochran's female pilots were as young as 18 and others had children.

After the impasse with Culp Hobby about inclusion with the WAACs, Jackie Cochran pushed aggressively that summer of 1943 for a single unit to control the activity of all women pilots. She wanted her own Women's Airforce. She made a big gain on August 5, 1943 when General Arnold announced that the WAFS and the WFTD graduates would be merged and named Women's Airforce Service Pilots (WASP) with Jacqueline Cochran as Director and Nancy Love as Executive of the Ferrying Division of the Air Transport Command (ATC). Prior to this, the WAFS and the WFTD had operated independently and without much interaction between their two rival leaders. Jean says, "As Betty Gillies (one of the original WAFS) so poignantly put it, 'We were WAFS until we woke up the morning of August 5, 1943 and learned that someone had changed our name while we slept. All WAFS were now WASP. We lost our Squadron Commander Nancy Love. We lost our wings. We lost our uniforms. We lost our identity.'" Some WAFS felt extremely bitter about this.

6: Graduation and AAF Air Transport Command Base Assignments

On August 7, 1943, Jean was one of 112 graduates out of 151 women in WFTD Class 43-4. Jean says, "Upon receiving our wings from Jackie Cochran at graduation, the custom was to trade your wings with someone else—perhaps it's just superstition that if you wear your own, bad luck may follow you. Not everyone does this. Three of us buddies made a three-way swap. We will never know whose wings we ended up with." (1)

Jean was 24 and officially a WASP, with the merger of WAFS and WFTD declared two days before her graduation. She was immediately sent to the ATC Ferrying Division at Daugherty Field in Long Beach, California. Jean says, "Betty Jane (B.J.) Erickson was our Squadron Leader at Long Beach. She was one of the youngest of the original 28 WAFS and younger than any of us at Long Beach but she handled her responsibilities like a pro." Jean knew five of the original WAFS – B.J. Erickson, Cornelia Fort, Betty Gillies, Nancy Love and Evelyn Sharp (Sharpie). At Long Beach, Jean had an appendicitis attack and the WASP had no access to a military hospital, health care, or health insurance. Her Uncle Irving in Santa Ana found a local doctor for her and she went to Long Beach Memorial Hospital. B.J. met her there and stayed until she was prepped for surgery. B.J. and Jean became lifelong friends.

At Long Beach ATC, Jean lived in the barracks on base with other WASP. She had a small private room with a bed, tall metal cabinet for clothes, chair and a desk where she put her prized red lamp from Aunt Lu. Jean ate in the enlisted men's mess for fifty cents a meal. On layovers, she stayed in the barracks on base for $1.50 a night instead of paying $5 a night for a motel. Jean says,

> None of the WAFS nor the graduates of WFTD had an official uniform at first. Our Long Beach ATC Ferrying Division decided to wear the Army olive green shirt, Army "pinks" for pants, khaki colored tie, overseas hat, and highly polished brown shoes. We really looked sharp! A tailor had to take in the waist of the smallest size men's pants and took the excess out at the back seam. This brought the back pockets very close together. During WFTD training, our flight suits were second-hand Army-issued mechanics coveralls that we nicknamed zoot suits. We rolled up the sleeves and put rubber bands or string on the pant legs to keep them off the ground.

Jean says, "At Long Beach, we ferried Training Planes: PTs, BTs, and ATs (Primary, Bomber and Advanced Trainers), up and down the West Coast. After a few months, it was decided that some of us should be trained to fly Fighter Planes." Jean was selected to go to Brownsville, Texas for the vigorous training on the elite Fighter Planes. She says, "The planes available for our one-month training were: P-40 Warhawk; P-47 Thunderbolt, and P-51 Mustang, among other planes. The P-47 weighed 7 tons, was sluggish, and when shot down, fell out of the sky like a bucket of bolts." Jean flew all of them and was one of only 130 women qualified to fly Fighter Planes.

During an early solo training flight in a P-51 Mustang, her instructor told her to take off, climb to pattern height, and then make a series of practice approaches, overshooting each time until she was confident she could land the aircraft. As she came back to the pattern, the gear-down light was red indicating unlocked landing gear. "I went through all of the procedures to correct it, but the red light remained on. Again and again, I dove down at high speed, then sharply pulled it back up hoping the force of gravity would snap the gear into place. Nothing worked so I called the tower for instruction for an emergency landing.

They said, 'It looks like the landing gear is down, come on in and try for a soft landing; gently touch your wheels to the runway to see if they hold.'

I said, OK, looked down and they had the Hash Wagon (Ambulance) and Fire Trucks ready for my emergency landing. This wasn't very encouraging to say the least. I gently bumped the wheels, they held, and I taxied in.

My instructor said, 'Well, what did you do wrong?'

I said, I thought I went through all of the emergency procedures, SIR! Later, my instructor went up in that plane and soon I saw him diving down, and then sharply snapping it back up a couple of times and I chuckled a little. He had the same problem. The malfunction was in the warning-light circuits." (1)

Jean says, "Flying a P-51 Mustang is like strapping on a pair of wings." This was her favorite of all the Fighter Planes. She liked its looks, its sound, its feel, and especially its power. "Cruising speed is 150 mph. It redlines at 300 mph and in those days it was the fastest plane we had. It could take a Japanese Zero with no questions asked. When you're flying in a P-51, you felt like a bird, like part of the plane." When Jean finished training in fighters at Brownsville, Texas she returned to Long Beach ATC and began ferrying P-51s from Inglewood, California where they were manufactured, to Newark, New Jersey where they were stowed on Liberty Ships for transport to the European fighting front. Altogether 15,682 Mustangs were built and in 1943 each one cost $58,824.

Jean was flying most of the time, and away from her home base more than she was there. They worked every day, sunup to sundown. After returning to the base from delivering a plane, she slept in her room, got up the next day and received her orders to deliver the next plane. The WASP took the "Recon Car" to Inglewood to pick up the next B-51 to be delivered. The car was like a station wagon that held 4 or 5 pilots. Jean says,

> The flight to Newark took ten hours; but in bad weather we might have to layover and could be stuck on a base for days. There was very little room in a P-51. I wore a 30-pound parachute and took a small satchel with my pajamas, toothbrush, shirt, maybe a skirt or dress and that became a pillow behind my back when I was in the cockpit. I stuck a second small satchel with harder things like high heels and cold cream in the ammunition compartment on the wing. I threw both satchels into my parachute bag when I flew back to Long Beach ATC.

6: Graduation and AAF Air Transport Command Base Assignments

The Flight Plan designated where and when pilots would stop for gas. Jean took no food or drink on her flights. She had no problem staying awake because "You were too busy staying on course using dead reckoning, being alert about weather, watching your altitude and approaching mountains, the sound of your engine, etc. etc. Who could possibly get sleepy?" They never flew at night. Jean loved crossing the mountains but always thought, "Where in HELL can I land this thing if it quits on me?"

Pilots carried a relief tube for urinating. Jean says, "It was hard for a woman to use as you first had to unlatch your safety belt, then the harness of your parachute, then unzip your coveralls, then your pants, try to stand halfway up to get in a position to get the cup of the relief tube where it belonged. You usually ended up wetting your pants." Jean says,

> There was little time for anyone to take family visits as they were cranking out P-51s pretty fast and all of them had to get to New Jersey quickly to be loaded onto Liberty Ships. Once in a while I asked for time off to visit my family in El Cajon. One time my car was being worked on so I hitchhiked home. My folks definitely did not approve of that and drove me the 120 miles back to the base!

> I was a cautious pilot and followed all the rules. One of the worst experiences I had was flying a P-51 to Newark, going 200 mph when I saw a shadow and then the belly of

another P-51 in my face. I thought that was it. I was furious that some smartass came up to scare me. We landed at the same base and he felt terrible and couldn't apologize enough. Since then, I never wanted anyone near me when I was flying and would not want to fly in formation.

Reactions to a woman climbing out of a P-51 were varied, but mostly startled. Once I had a slight mechanical problem so I called in and asked for permission to land. I kept radioing P-51 ready to land, awaiting final landing instructions. It was sort of garbled and they kept asking me to call in again and again.

Finally they said, 'Waggle your wings if you receive.'

So there I was waggling away and pretty soon they came back 'Lady, the only thing we see up there is a P-51. Where are you?'

I replied, 'That's me. I am the P-51.' They couldn't believe it, they were looking for a Piper Cub or something. Finally, when I landed, what a welcome I got. Word got around that a gal was flying that thing. By the time I had taxied up to the line, following the little "Follow Me" truck, there were lots of guys around to see what kind of woman was flying this P-51. They'd never heard of us, the WASP. (1)

After delivering a P-51 to Newark New Jersey I would frequently be assigned to pick up either a Bell Aircraft P-39 Cobra or the

> beefed up P-63 King Cobra at the factory in
> Buffalo, New York, to be delivered to Great
> Falls, Montana. A military pilot would then
> fly the aircraft to Alaska because we were not
> militarized yet and were forbidden to fly
> across the borders of the U.S.A. The Russian
> pilots, some of them women, would pick
> them up in Alaska (Appendix F) and take
> them to the fighting front. This was a Lend-
> Lease Agreement whereby equipment and
> services were provided for countries fighting
> Germany. If there were no Bell Aircraft
> planes to be delivered, I was put on a
> commercial airliner back to Los Angeles.
> They gave WASP preference over almost
> everyone else and would bump others to get
> us back to our ferrying responsibilities. I
> always wore my uniform and coveralls as
> there was no time to change clothes. (1)

On one of Jean's flights from Long Beach to
Newark, New Jersey in a brand new P-51 Mustang,
she let her El Cajon family know she was going to
buzz the house. "The family heard me coming and
were all out on the front lawn waving. I flew just
above the hilltops, telephone and electric lines. I
buzzed it again, waggled my wings a couple of
times and headed east to Palm Springs. It was
risky. If they had caught me, they probably would
have grounded me." Jean says,

> One morning I was in the 'Ready Room' in
> Newark, New Jersey waiting for orders and
> noticed an unfamiliar fighter plane out on
> the line. ATC (Air Traffic Control) said, 'Go
> sit in the cockpit, become familiar with the

location of all the gauges, read the emergency procedures, and if you feel comfortable, go ahead and ask the tower for takeoff instructions.' I did that, and headed for Great Falls, Montana. When I arrived I called for landing instructions and all went well until final approach. When I lowered the flaps at the appropriate time, it felt like the plane dropped out from under me and assumed an unusual steep, slow glide, like a bird fluttering down getting ready to land on the branch of a tree. I could see I would never make it to the runway with this strange glide so I aborted the landing—up with the flaps, up with the landing gear, and went around again. This time, I got considerably closer to the runway before applying the flaps and landed with no problem. When I asked one of the mechanics about this strange reaction to the flaps he said, 'Oh, that's a Navy plane and it's designed to land on Navy carriers. The flaps have rather large holes in them which allows the plane to come in at a slower pace and uses up less runway before it is hooked and brought to a stop on the deck of a ship.'

It would have been nice if someone had told me ahead of time to watch out about the strange reaction to the flaps. (1)

7: WASP Responsibilities Expand to Release Men for Air War U.S. is Losing

In early 1944, Jean was selected to go to Rosecrans Army Airfield in St. Joseph, Missouri for a month of four-engine bomber training as a co-pilot on the Boeing B-17 Flying Fortress and the Douglas C-47 military transport aircraft that carried troops and up to 6,000 pounds of cargo.

By September 1943 it was obvious that Jacqueline Cochran's WFTD graduates were far more than the four ATC Ferrying Posts could absorb. Cochran and General Arnold decided to send most of the graduates to some of the 120 Army Air Bases in the U.S. to take the place of military pilots who were doing all kinds of flying jobs that women could handle – such as towing targets, laying smoke screens for practice, and performing searchlight and tracking missions. This would release hundreds of male fighter and bomber pilots to go to the fighting front. The women, for the most part were well received, did an excellent job, and released men badly needed to win the air war we were losing.

However, WASP were not always welcomed at some of the bases. At Camp Davis, North Carolina, some of the 25 women thought it was clear the men did not want them there. Some of the men were worried that the women would replace them and they would be shipped overseas for combat duty. The women towed targets to give ground and air gunners training shooting with live ammunition. Many planes assigned to WASP had been returned from combat duty and were in need of repair. Women pilots experienced repeated engine failures. They expressed concern that the planes were not being properly maintained but no one listened.

Jean says, "There were stories of sabotage with sugar in gas tanks, sand in carburetors, even cut rudder cables. There were no official investigations as Jackie Cochran thought that would create bad publicity for the women pilots military inclusion. You just accepted it or quit."

8: Killed in the Service of Her Country

The first death of a WFTD Trainee was on March 7, 1943 at Houston, Texas. Margaret Oldenburg, a classmate of Jean's, and her instructor Norris Morgan were killed flying a PT-19 about six miles south of Houston Army Air Field. Oldenburg was the 33-year-old wife of a Navy Ensign. The plane was "out of rig", Form 1-A showed it was restricted to non-aerobatic maneuvers and they were doing spins. Form 1-A was a flight report kept day-to-day noting: time flown, total hours, pilot, aerial engineer, radio operator, condition of the plane, gas added, station and other data.

Cornelia Fort died two weeks after Oldenburg on March 21, 1943. She was 24 years old and one of the original 28 WAFS. Fort was ferrying BT-13's to Love Field in Dallas, Texas when one of the male pilots assigned to the same mission flew too close to her plane and his landing gear clipped her airplane's left wing, and sent it plummeting to earth with no time to parachute to safety. She had been flying for her country for just five months. Her Commanding Officer, Nancy Love wrote Fort's mother: "My feeling about the loss of Cornelia is hard to put into words—I can only say that I miss her terribly, and loved her.... If there can be any comforting thought, it is that she died as she wanted to—in an Army airplane, and in the service of her country." Her epitaph reads "Killed in the Service of Her Country".

When Pearl Harbor was bombed, Cornelia Fort was a Civilian Pilot Instructor at John Rodgers Airport (next to Pearl Harbor), and was in the air with one of her students practicing takeoffs and landings. Fort wrote an article describing what happened, "At the twilight's last gleaming" in *Women's Home*

Companion and published posthumously in July of 1943. The article was prefaced with "…. her words here will live—as a moving account of why one woman joined the WAFS and as a testament to all American women who are helping keep America free."

Fort writes that she saw a military plane coming directly toward them, grabbed the controls from her student and jammed the throttle wide open to pull above the oncoming plane. She looked down and saw the red Japanese Rising Sun symbol on top of the Zero's wings. Next she saw billows of black smoke at Pearl Harbor. Then she saw "the formation of silver bombers riding in. Something detached itself from an airplane and came glistening down" and exploded in the middle of the harbor. She landed quickly, began to taxi back to the hangar when a shadow passed over and bullets spattered all around her. She and others counted their civilian Cub planes as they landed and two never came back. They washed ashore weeks later on the windward side of the island, bullet-riddled. Fort returned to the United States three months later and became an Instructor for the Civilian Pilot Training Program (CPTP).

Fort wrote in her logbook, "Flight interrupted by Japanese attack on Pearl Harbor. An enemy plane shot at my plane and missed and proceeded to strafe John Rodgers, a civilian airport. Another plane machine gunned the ground in front of me as I taxied to the hangar."

In September 1942, Fort received a telegram from U.S. War Secretary Henry Stinson announcing the organization of the WAFS to serve in the Ferrying Division of the Army Air Force (AAF) Air Transport

Command at Wilmington, Delaware. If she was interested in flying military planes, she had to report in 24 hours and she left immediately.

In the *Women's Home Companion* article Cornelia Fort wrote, "We are beginning to prove that women can be trusted to deliver airplanes safely and in the doing serve the country which is our country too. I have yet to have a feeling which approaches in satisfaction that of having signed, sealed and delivered an airplane for the United States Army.... I, for one, am profoundly grateful that my one talent, my only knowledge, flying, happens to be of use to my country when it is needed. That's all the luck I ever hope to have"

On April 3, 1944, Jean's friend Evelyn "Sharpie" Sharp was killed on her way to Newark with a new twin-engine Lockheed P-38 Lightening, a twin-engine fuselage aircraft. Sharpie was a 24-year-old barnstorming pilot from Nebraska, flying at county fairs and rodeos where she took people up, often for their first plane rides. She was one of the original 28 WAFS. Jean remembers, "She was on takeoff from Harrisburg, Pennsylvania, full throttle, both engines at high RPM. She became airborne for only a brief moment when her left engine quit. The torque of the other powerful engine caused the plane to turn, roll, go down, and crash. There is very little a pilot can do about it." (1)

A close friend of Sharpie's and Jean's, B.J. Erickson, Squadron Commander at Long Beach said, "I was at a meeting in Cincinnati with Nancy (Love) when it came in over the teletype that the P-38 has crashed at Harrisburg and it was a WASP pilot and there were only three or four of us flying

38's at that particular point... I knew almost who it had to be. And she was probably one of the best pilots we had. She lost an engine on takeoff on a runway that was short, going towards a hill, and she controlled it as best she could but she pancaked into the hill and was killed instantly." Sharpie "got her flying time in at Lone Pine, California, instructing. She was very outgoing, very gregarious; she loved to date—was very attractive and didn't have an enemy in the world. She was everybody's friend ... and an excellent pilot. She was very quick to learn ... very upbeat and very capable."

Thirty-eight Women That Died as WWII Pilots for the
Air Force (findagrave.com)

Name / City	Age
Jane Delores Champlin St. Louis, Missouri	26
Susan Parker Clarke Cooperstown, New York	25
Margie Laverne Davis Hollywood, California	21
Katherine M. Applegate Dussaq Dayton, Washington	39
Marjorie Doris Edwards Fullerton, California	25
Elizabeth "Jayne" Erickson Seattle, Washington	22
Cornelia Clark Fort Nashville, Tennessee	24
Frances Fortune Grimes Pittsburgh, Pennsylvania	29
Mary P. Hartson Portland, Oregon	27
Mary Holmes Howson Valley Forge, Pennsylvania	25

Name / City	Age
Edith "Edy" Clayton Keene Pomona, California	23
Kathryn "Kay" Barbara Lawrence Grand Forks, North Dakota	22
Paula Ruth Loop Wakita, Oklahoma	27
Alice E. Lovejoy Hartsdale, New York	29
Peggy Wilson Martin Whittier, California	32
Lea Ola McDonald Seagraves, Texas	22
Virginia Caraline Moffatt Inglewood, California	31
Beverly Jean Moses Pleasant Hill, Iowa	21
Dorothy "Dottie" Mae Nichols Glendale, California	27
Jeanne Marcile Lewellen Norbeck Columbus, Indiana	31
Margaret B. Sanford Oldenburg Oakland, California	33

8: Killed in the Service of Her Country

Name / City	Age
Mabel Virginia Rawlinson Kalamazoo, Michigan	26
Gleanna Roberts Johnson County, Iowa	25
Marie N. Michell Robinson Troy, Michigan	20
Dorothy Faeth Scott North Hollywood, California	23
Elizabeth "Bettie" Mae Scott Monrovia, California	22
Margaret "Peggy" June Seip Milwaukee, Wisconsin	27
Helen Jo Anderson Severson Brookings, South Dakota	24
Marie Ethel Cihler Sharon Portland, Oregon	26
Evelyn "Sharpie" Genevieve Sharp Ord, Nebraska	24
Gertrude "Tommy" Tompkins Silver Jersey City, New Jersey	32
Betty Pauline Stine Santa Barbara, California	22

Name / City	Age
Marian J. Toevs Aberdeen, Idaho	26
Mary Elizabeth Trebing Boulder, Colorado	22
Mary Louise Webster Ellensburg, Washington	25
Bonnie Jean Alloway Welz San Jose, California	26
Betty Louise Taylor Wood Sacramento, California	22
Hazel Ying Lee Yim-Qun Portland, Oregon	32

9: Militarization of the WASP and Jean Reports to Officer Candidate School

February 1944
WASP Militarization Legislation

In Jacqueline Cochran's "Final WASP Report" (Appendix G), she gives the following rationale for WASP militarization.

> An act of Congress was necessary to place the WASP on military status as a part of the Army Air Forces. The program was started on a civilian basis in the belief that it should be tested first as to its potentialities before taking decision as to desirability of militarization. It was known that the women ferry pilots in England were employed by British Overseas Airways and were put under term contract, which carried $10,000 insurance benefits at no cost to the pilot and which not only assured service after transition training, but also contained stipulation dealing with controls and off-duty discipline. Such term contracts were not found possible here. The training program could be and was set up along military lines, even though the personnel was not militarized.

> With comparatively few women pilots on operational duty until the fore part of 1943, the need for early militarization was not urgent, and in the beginning the writer (Jacqueline Cochran) recommended that the question of militarization be deferred until enough experience had been obtained to determine the usefulness of the women

pilots to the AAF. But, with graduates of
Sweetwater being assigned in large numbers
to operating stations, it became increasingly
evident that the best results from the women
pilot program could not be obtained unless
the WASP could be governed, directed, and
treated as a part of the Air Force personnel.
They were flying the same as AAF flying
officers on domestic assignments but were
not subject to the same rules. They were
living at AAF bases, dealing with Air Force
equipment, eating in officer's mess rooms,
and associating with flying personnel, and
yet were governed by an entirely different set
of laws and regulations. They did not have
any progressive schedule of advancement or
pay. They had no Government insurance. It
was difficult to work out for them even
hospitalization in case of sickness or
accident, and to have them hospitalized
elsewhere than in AAF hospitals under the
supervision of flight surgeons would have
prevented any sound approach to the
experimental features of the program. They
could resign at any time with or without just
cause, which made weak any coordinated
control in matters dealing with discipline,
welfare, and health.

These and many similar considerations
caused a decision to be reached early in
1944 to recommend to Congress
militarization of the WASP. A bill to that end
was favorably reported out by the Military
Affairs Committee of the House of
Representatives. (2)

9: Militarization of the WASP and Jean Reports to Officer Candidate School

General Hap Arnold Addresses WASP Graduation Class 44-2

WASP Class 44-2 graduated on March 13, 1944 in their new official Santiago Blue uniforms. In anticipation of militarization, General Arnold told the graduates, "I'm looking forward to the day when Women Airforce Service Pilots take the place of practically all the male pilots of the Army Air Force in this country for the duration. Indeed, this organization has come to serve a variety of useful purposes in the Army Air Forces organization. We're proud of you and we welcome you as a part of the Army Air Forces."

Secretary of War Henry L. Stimson sent a letter of support for the long promised militarization of WASP (HR 3358) in February 1944. California Representative John Martin Costello submitted a longer bill (HR 4219) to make the WASP a women's service within the U.S. Army Air Force. The previous bill was first introduced in September 1941 and ignored by Congress.

On March 24, 1944 the Senate Bill to militarize WASP within the Army Air Force was introduced and WASP were told they will soon be commissioned and must go through Officer Candidate School (OCS). The House Military Affairs Committee had issued a report recommending passage of HR4219 and General Arnold requested commissions for WASP. On April 19 the first class of 50 WASP, including Nancy Love, entered OCS at the AAF School of Applied Tactics in Orlando, Florida to prepare to be officers. Many classes were co-ed and others were for WASP only. They graduated on May 12, 1944. Jean was selected to attend the second WASP class to report for Officer Candidate School.

10: June 1944 European War Winds Down

By the summer of 1944 General Hap Arnold was with General Dwight Eisenhower in Europe directing air operations and coordinating battle plans for the top-secret D-Day landing on Normandy Beaches. On June 6, 1944 the allied invasion to liberate Europe from Nazi occupation began just after midnight. This was the largest invasion force in history and included: more than 160,000 allied troops (about half Americans) landing at Normandy, 4,000 invasion ships, 600 warships, and more than 13,000 planes. Allied pilots flew approximately 15,000 sorties on D-Day. There were: 4,414 fatalities—2,499 were American, and 1,915 fatalities were from the Allied nations.

The European war seemed to be winding down and some thought the pilot shortage was over. The male Civilian Pilot's Lobby began an anti-WASP campaign because their flight training programs were closing down and they wanted the WASP jobs. The media, most notably Drew Pearson, a Washington Post gossip columnist, demanded WASP deactivation in several of his newspaper columns. A Time magazine article on May 29, 1944 titled "Unnecessary and Undesirable" calls the WASP experiment expensive and claims men could have been trained more quickly. Secretary of War Stimson ordered the WASP not to respond to the vicious printed attacks. The WASP evidently could release men for duty, but could not replace them. And the truth of their value and the country's need for these experienced pilots was not acknowledged.

June 21, 1944 WASP Militarization Bill Defeated and Deactivation Ordered

Two weeks after D-Day on June 21, 1944, the WASP Militarization Bill HR 4219 was defeated in Congress by just 19 votes, 188 to 169. Five days later, the House Report recommended immediate discontinuance of the WASP Training Program except for those already in training. WASP Class 45-1 started reporting to Avenger Field but the women had to return home at their own expense. There were 703 women in training in Classes 44-5 through 44-10. Of these, 365 (52%) completed their training and reported to one of the 19 duty bases. The last class served only ten days. There were 338 (48%) women who chose to return home.

WASP "become pilot material in excess of needs"

General Arnold ordered WASP discontinued as of December 20, 1944. On October 1, 1944, General Arnold sent the following memo to Jackie Cochran stating that because of the changing war situation the WASP would "soon become pilot material in excess of needs."

Headquarters, Army Air Forces, Washington

1 October 1944

SUBJECT: Deactivation of WASP
TO: Director of Women Pilots

1. The reduction in the flying training program and the changing war situation's bearing on the availability and deployment of pilots make it evident that the WASP will soon become pilot material in excess of needs.

2. The WASPs have well met the situation for which the women pilot program was activated. They have ably and loyally supplemented our activities during a time when a pilot shortage would have impaired the Air Forces' performance of its mission. They have served long enough to provide valuable data concerning their capabilities and versatility as a basis for future planning. They are serving, however, to release male pilots for other work and not to replace them. The time has arrived to plan the program's deactivation.

3. I have therefore directed that WASP be deactivated as soon as consistent with giving adequate advance notice to the WASPs and to the Commanding Officers of the bases where they are employed, and that you submit promptly to me your plan for such deactivation to take place not later than 29 December 1944.

4. In bringing to a close this important program of the Army Air Forces, I wish to express my appreciation to you for your resourceful, imaginative and tireless work. The success of the WASP Program is due in large measure to your contribution as its director.

H.H. ARNOLD
General, U.S. Army
Commanding General, Army Air Forces (2)

On October 3, 1944, Jacqueline Cochran sent a letter to all 916 active-duty WASP to inform them of the program's pending deactivation as of December 20, 1944. WASP were invited to resign in good standing until November 20. The War Department announced that the decision to disband the WASP was based on indications that by the end of the year, there would be sufficient male pilots to fill flying assignments in the U.S. and overseas.

General Arnold Addresses Final WASP Graduation Class 44-10

The following are excerpts from General Arnold's December 7, 1944 address to WASP Graduation Class 44-10.

You and more than 900 of your sisters have shown that you can fly wingtip to wingtip with your brothers. If ever there was any doubt in anyone's mind that women can become skillful pilots, the WASP have dispelled that doubt. Frankly, I didn't know in 1941 whether a slip of a young girl could fight the controls of a B-17 in heavy weather .... (N)ow in 1944, more than two years since WASP first started flying with the Air Forces, we can come to only one conclusion—the entire operation has been a success. It is on the record that women can fly as well as men .... I want to stress how valuable I believe this whole WASP program has been for the country .... We will know that they can handle our fastest fighters, our heaviest bombers .... So, on this last graduation day, I salute you and all WASP. We of the Army Air Force are proud of you; we will never forget our debt to you. (2)

10: *June 1944 European War Winds Down*

General Arnold Letter to all WASP

The WASP became part of the Air Forces because we had to explore the nation's total manpower resources and in order to release male pilots for other duties. Their very successful record of accomplishment has proved that in any future total effort the nation can count on thousands of its young women to fly any of its aircraft. You have freed male pilots for other work, but now the war situation has changed and the time has come when your volunteered services are no longer needed. The situation is that, if you continue in service, you will be replacing instead of releasing our young men. I know that the WASP wouldn't want that. So, I have directed that the WASP program be inactivated and all WASP be released on 20 December 1944. I want you to know that I appreciate your war service and that the Army Air Force will miss you. I also know that you will join us in being thankful that our combat losses have proved to be much lower than anticipated, even though it means inactivation of the WASP.

Jean had completed AAF Officer Candidate School and was expecting militarization of the WASP while the anti-WASP campaign gathered momentum. She was shocked at the betrayal and heartbroken to lose the job she loved so dearly, and under false pretenses as described by Brigadier General Nowland, Commander of the ATC Ferrying Division. In a "Secret Memorandum" dated November 1, 1944 to the Commanding General of the ATC, Hap Arnold, Brigadier General Nowland wrote, "The announced inactivation of the WASP ... will have a profound effect on the ability of the Ferrying Division to meet its commitments and to deliver pursuit type aircraft." He said, it was planned to keep 117 WASPs permanently on pursuit deliveries to release men for progressive upgrading to meet foreign quotas. Replacing the experienced WASPs with male pilots entails a month's training at Brownsville costing over one million dollars total and a minimum of 4 months experience to insure effective utilization. Each male pilot has to be among the more experienced pilots since a minimum of 400 hours and an instrument card are necessary prerequisites for pursuit training and safe delivery of fighters. WASP have been specializing in this type of flying for 18 months and the male pilots will not be as efficient due to lack of experience.

General Arnold is said to have replied, "Evaluation of this program in terms of dollars and cents is not the immediate issue at stake and personnel under your control should scrupulously avoid any discussion along this line."

Jean was one of the expert and irreplaceable 117 WASP flying pursuit aircraft. She was continuously ferrying P-51 Mustangs, a single-seat, long-range escort fighter, from Inglewood, California to Newark, New Jersey. The men replacing the WASP pilots would need months of training and experience, and would cost more since they received higher wages than women, and flight pay, and benefits that were not given to the women pilots.

10: June 1944 European War Winds Down

WASP Records Sealed, Classified, and Stored for over 33 Years

The WASP story was missing from United States history books because the government sealed, classified and stored the records making them unavailable to historians. Many of the records were not declassified until the 1980s.

WASP paid their own way to enter training and had to pay their own way back home. Until June 1944, the WASP believed they would be granted military status. It never occurred to them they would end their service to the Air Force as civilians with no piloting career opportunities, honors or benefits.

The government betrayal of the WASP by denying the promised militarization and commissioning as Second Lieutenants was a stunning blow. Losing the job they loved was devastating and heartbreaking. WASP knew they were needed to continue ferrying planes they were trained to fly and most men were not trained to fly. Jean and other WASP at the Long Beach ATC "wrote telegrams to President Roosevelt, General Arnold and others, offering to fly throughout the winter at least, for $1.00 a year. We received a very nice commendation, but deactivation came anyway. Here we were in a war; they needed us desperately, and we were deactivated at the wrong moment." WASP anger at the AAF rejection and the major injustice by Congress set in. Jean and other WASP looked for alternative opportunities to fly with America's allies. They wrote letters inquiring about military pilot jobs in England and China. Jean told her parents and received the following letter from her father.

Letter to Jean from Her father
November 8, 1944

My dear Jean:

I have read your letter of October 27 a number of times and have carried it in my pocket for some days, waiting an opportunity to write you about some of the things it contains and some of the thoughts it brings to mind.

Your expressed disappointment at the probable fate of the WASP, the happiness you have derived from ferrying pursuits and the prospect of ending this association, especially with the P-51 lets us know your deep concern. The fact that we have not previously known, that you, along with some others, had written to both England and China, inquiring about possible pilot duties with either of these countries tells us with strong emphasis your disappointment at the attitude of this government, and your intent to continue military flying for the duration of the war if at all possible.

I have expressed to you my own dissatisfaction at the manner in which the WASP are being treated. You can well imagine that the suggestion of your accepting service in aviation with the Air Corps of any other nation has prompted me to much thought.

I feel intensely that you should have been commissioned in the Army Air Force immediately upon graduation from Sweetwater. Since that was not done and the WASP are now to be inactivated, nothing less than a commission effective the day before you are released can save the government from shame. But even though this is not done, I feel that I should caution you in regard to serious consideration of service with the forces of any other nation. I have only the highest respect for your desire to go on.

However, my dear, there is a grave difference between serving your country in war or in joining the ranks of another, even an ally.

The one is the urge of patriotism, the other is too often, the desire for adventure. The world has never accorded to the soldier of fortune, the honor or esteem that it gives the patriot.

Love, Dad

Others might see Jean as patriotic and heroic in volunteering to fly for an ally fighting the same enemy as our country. Jean says,

Most everyone I knew would have gone into combat had that been allowed. But it did not come to pass. I'd heard that the Russians allowed women in combat. They were so feared by the Germans that they were dubbed the 'Night Witches'. (1) (Appendix F)

Jean's most memorable WASP moment was also her saddest, dipping the wings of her

P-51 Mustang as a salute to the Statue of Liberty, moments before landing at Newark, New Jersey for the last time! If you did that today, you'd be shot down. I circled the Statue of Liberty a couple of times and wept. I wept. We paid for our own transportation home. There were no provisions made to get us home, no thanks, no one said anything, that was the end of it. (1)

Male pilots conducted an effective campaign against the WASP, arguing that the women weren't needed. Jean says, "Some of the brass thought we would be taking jobs that should go to the returning male pilots. We thought there were jobs for all of us and we could work together. There were P-51s and other planes just sitting on airfields with nobody to fly them."

Deactivation of the WASP was costly for both the war effort and taxpayers. It deprived the ATC of hundreds of expert ferrying pilots, tow target pilots, test pilots, and administrative pilots. It cost a million dollars to train men to replace the women, and it hampered the delivery of planes during the four to six months necessary to train men. It also prevented men who were being transferred to ferry duty from completing training for specialized combat missions. Women pilots beginning with the WAFS had 2 years of flying experience that could not be replaced. The WASP did half of the pursuit ferrying in the United States. WASP were trained on many different aircraft whereas male pilots were usually trained on fewer planes, whatever was available at their base before they were sent to the fighting front.

Jean says,

> Six months after D-Day in December 1944, the male pilots came home. Jackie Cochran was tired of being a civilian, gave up fighting for militarization and the need for trained WASP pilots, and that spelled the end of the WASP. She wanted her own military command and wasn't going to get it. She wanted to be her own leader through the WAC. We were deactivated when the war was still on and they still needed us. (1)

As civilians, the WASP received no health insurance, no burial or death benefits, no military rank, and no access to programs such as Veterans

Home Loans or GI Bill benefits for education. There was no Gold Star in the window or flag draped over the coffin when a female pilot died flying military planes. Her funeral was not paid for by the U.S. Government and her friends on base often had to pass a hat to pay to ship her body and belongings home by train with a WASP escort. In contrast, women serving in other branches of the military, WAC, WAVES, SPARS, and Marines, were militarized, and had all the benefits.

All told, 350,000 women served in the U.S. armed forces during WWII, beginning in December 1941.

1945 Post WASP — From Flying to Teaching

Jean says,

> Immediately after WASP deactivation, while looking for a teaching position, I took one and only one brief flying job. We were to fly some old open-cockpit Boeing Stearman Biplanes 1200 miles from Wickenburg, Arizona to Portland, Oregon. They had been 'stored' out in the sun, wind, and rain for years; labeled 'for storage only.' Mine barely got off the ground and when trying to land at the first stop in Blythe, California, the engine quit cold. I wiped out the only electric wires leading into town—total darkness that night. They replaced a few spark plugs the next morning and I was on my way again. Crossing over the high mountains to Portland, Oregon, the carburetor froze up and so did my hands and face. I sat on one hand or chewed on it to try to warm it and

keep circulation flowing. I flew as low as I safely could and worried about the carburetor freezing again. The old 'clunker' sputtered a few times but kept going. I was oh, so glad to reach Portland. Having flown the greatest fighter in the world at that time, the P-51 Mustang, this experience was not high on my list of things to do again. (1)

A few WASP found piloting jobs after the war, but none of the major airlines would hire female pilots. Some scored groundwork with the AAF and with manufacturers and airlines.

Jean had taken a "Military Leave of Absence" from her teaching position at Grossmont High School in El Cajon, California, but since WASP were not militarized as was promised, Grossmont did not hold her position.

The G.I. Bill was signed by President Franklin Roosevelt in June 1944, just days after the D-Day invasion of Normandy. Colleges were hiring teachers to meet the demand for the large numbers of veterans who were enrolling. In 1945 Jean was hired by Park College in Parkville, Missouri to teach Health, Physical Education and Recreation. She took a one-year Leave of Absence from Park College in 1947 to earn a masters degree at Wellesley College in Massachusetts.

In 1949, Jean was 30 and teaching at Park College when she met and married Charles H. White, a 43-year-old physician who lived across the River in Kansas City, Kansas, They divorced three years later. In 1950, Jean accepted a position in Pennsylvania at West Chester State Teacher's College and taught there for almost ten years.

11: WASP Reaction to Deactivation and the Aftermath

From 1959 to 1969 Jean taught in Muncie, Indiana at Ball State Teachers College, and then made a final move back to her alma mater San Diego State University where she taught until she retired in 1979.

WWII Pilot, Betrayal, Then Congressional Gold Medal

12: 1977 WASP Mobilize for Militarization

With the 1977 spurious U.S. Defense Department announcement that for the first time in our nation's history women would be permitted to fly military planes, the outraged WASP mobilized in order to gain the recognition long overdue, acknowledging their service and place in history. The WASP had powerful opposition once again, this time from: the Veterans of Foreign Wars, Veterans Administration, President Jimmy Carter, and the American Legion who said WASP militarization "would denigrate the term 'veteran' so that it will never again have the value that presently attaches to it."

Patricia Collins Hughes, WASP 44-6, was a columnist for *The Stars and Stripes—The National Tribune.* She advocated for WASP to receive veteran's status and a discharge based on the same criteria used to qualify men in the same Military Occupational Specialty during WWII. Her October 6, 1977 column was titled (President) "Carter Fails on Campaign Promise" and says that the AAF recruited licensed experienced women pilots when they needed an air force overnight. Collins Hughes makes the case that "the only way to keep this country's forces at their present level of approximately 2 million ... short of returning to the draft ... is to enlist more women. As things now stand, there would be places for 400,000 of them; any more than that, and it would be necessary to let women be combat soldiers."

She quoted William Randolph Hearst, Jr., Editor-in-chief of The Hearst Newspapers, "The total cost to the Republic to provide full veteran rights to the brave women who served their country so well more than a quarter of a century ago would be a measly $100,000 per year for as long as the 850 survivors remain in our midst. Not a hundred million, not even one million, but 100 thousand."

"To resist this on grounds of its cost is nothing short of incredible for an administration that is requesting $10.6 billion for the first year's budget for its new Department of Energy." She ends with "It is simply not proper to deprive them of the military benefits that were bestowed by a grateful populace on all other military personnel."

Arizona Senator Barry Goldwater, a WWII veteran who had flown with WASP aviators in the ATC offered powerful support to the WASP, along with the Department of Defense, Colonel Bruce Arnold (General Hap Arnold's son), Representative Margaret Heckler of Massachusetts, Representative Lindy Boggs of Louisiana, and the military news weekly *Stars and Stripes*. The WASP veterans made their case to Congress describing their: military training, top-secret missions, drills, uniforms and sidearms that made them a military rather than a civilian organization.

Byrd Howell Granger, a former WASP Commanding Officer, compiled a dossier of more than 100 pages of documents showing that the WASP were: subject to military discipline, assigned to top secret missions, and many of them received service ribbons after their units were disbanded. One document more than any other was especially persuasive, an "Honorable Discharge" certificate granted to WASP Helen Porter by her Commanding Officer at Strother Field in Kansas. It said, "This is to certify that Helen Porter honorably served in active Federal Service in the Army of the United

States." This same wording was used in 1944 for all honorable discharges in the Army.

1977 WASP Finally Militarized

Congress finally recognized WASP service as active duty in the armed forces that entitled them to veteran's benefits 33 years later in 1977. They lifted the ban and granted the WASP full veterans status. President Carter signed a bill into law "Officially declaring the Women Airforce Service Pilots as having served on active duty in the Armed Force of the United States for purposes of laws administered by the Veterans Administration." However, these heroic women were not invited to President Carter's signing ceremony at the White House on November 23, 1977. Further insult occurred when the Department of the Air Force did not authorize official discharges for WASP until more than a year later on March 8, 1979. Then in May 1979, the Air Force issued the first honorable discharge for women serving as WASP during WWII. Adding to this injustice, it was not until 1984, seven years after the Congressional action, that a WWII Victory Medal and an American Campaign Medal were mailed to WASP in a plain brown envelope with no letter. WASP Records were finally released and made available to historians and the general public. One veteran said, "We were finally recognized for what we had done (over) thirty years before." Another veteran added that the measure "gave the families of the girls that were killed a feeling that they died for their country." The victory also meant that a few days after Congress' decision, Colonel Arnold could tell a WASP that she could and should put the Stars and Stripes on the grave of a WASP colleague to commemorate Veterans Day. They received no back pay or death insurance.

Women were again permitted to attend military pilot training in the United States Armed Forces. Thousands of female aviators flying support aircraft have benefited from the service of the WASP and followed in their footsteps.

13: 2009 Congressional Gold Medal
Awarded to WASP

The greatest honor bestowed upon the WASP occurred in July 2009, when the U.S. Congress passed a bill to award the Congressional Gold Medal (the highest Congressional honor for civilians) to all WASP. On March 10, 2010, about 200 of these female aviators, mostly in their late 80s and early 90s and some in wheelchairs, came to the Capitol to accept the Medal from President Barack Obama. Senators Kay Bailey Hutchison (R-Texas) and Barbara Mikulski (D-Maryland), along with Representatives Ileana Ros-Lehtinen (R-Florida) and Susan Davis (D-California), led the effort in Congress to get the women recognized with the Congressional Gold Medal.

During the ceremony President Obama said, "The Women's Airforce Service Pilots courageously answered their country's call in a time of need while blazing a trail for the brave women who have given and continue to give so much in service to this nation since. Every American should be grateful for their service, and I am honored to sign this bill to finally give them some of the hard-earned recognition they deserve."

Jean did not go to Washington and received her medal from Colonel Laurel Scott in a ceremony at the El Cajon Airport with family and close friends, captured in the DVD "She Wore Silver Wings". Colonel Scott said, "On behalf of a grateful nation, we thank you for your services." (1)

14: Jean's Later Years

Retirement and Travel

During Jean's travels she fell in love with Bonners Ferry, Idaho on the Kootenai River, nestled between the Selkirk and sharp-peaked Cabinet Mountains. She bought five acres 30 miles from the Canadian border, and built a house that became her home for half of every year after she retired from teaching. The small town with around 2,000 people was a paradise of lakes, rivers, waterfalls and wildlife. She lived part time in this quiet solitude until she turned 92 in 2010 and sold. Now she lives full time in her El Cajon home with a little gray rescue dog Tammy. Tammy is totally blind and has trouble walking. Jean says, "She may ignore 'come' 'sit' 'stay' but she can hear a cookie drop in the kitchen." Jean, along with Tammy visit old friends in Rancho Mirage. Her sister-in-law lives nearby and calls every morning at 8 am. Jean recently stopped walks with Tammy because the sidewalks are terrible, the tree roots make them too dangerous. She also recently had to give up swimming 3 or 4 times a week because of a balance problem. Jean is an ardent environmentalist, especially concerned about the dangers of climate change. At 100, she remains independent and active, and still loves to garden.

Jean has "traveled abroad and toured our beautiful U.S. of A. by air, land, sea and especially in my RV." Her last faculty post was at her Alma Mater, San Diego State, where she held the position of Assistant Professor of Physical Education from 1969 to 1979. She was awarded the status of Emeritus Professor of Exercise and Nutritional

Science upon her retirement in 1979 after 37 years of teaching.

Jean's family surprised her in 2009 with a flight in a P-51 Mustang with Pilot Chuck Hall. He owned an Airport in Ramona, California, not far from El Cajon. There is only one seat in a pursuit fighter plane so he removed the auxiliary gas tank to make room for a passenger. Jean was glad he had a ladder to get her up there; but she didn't need one in the old days when she could just step up on the wing, even wearing a 30 pound parachute. There's a place in the wing's ammunition compartment where she used to stow her high heels and said, "At the end of some days, we liked to dress up and go out." Chuck did rolls to the left and to the right. Jean said, "I felt like a bird again. Loved the whole ride. This was a wonderful day I'll never forget. WOW what a ride." (1)

Jean's WASP experience was documented in the award winning 2010 DVD "She Wore Silver Wings" by her Grand Nephew Devin Scott and wife Jeanne Scott. This sparked a demand for Jean as a public speaker. She made presentations about her experiences as a WASP to Historical Societies, church groups, service clubs, and high school history classes. She especially loved speaking to "The Ninety-Nines", an International Organization of Women Pilots established in 1929 by 99 female pilots with Amelia Earhart as their first President.

Jean was further honored when she was selected to receive a 2015 Monty Award at San Diego State University. This Award is given to alumni as a symbol of achievement and success, and to honor those who have made significant contributions.

Lifelong WASP Friendships with B.J. Erickson
London and Ginny Hill Wood

Jean maintained a lifelong friendship with B.J. Erickson, her Squadron Commander at Long Beach until B.J. died at 93 in 2013. They both were close to WASP Ginny Wood who died the same year at 95, four months before B.J.

Profile of "B.J." Erickson London

Jean served under Barbara Jane Erickson's command at Long Beach ATC for her entire 16 months of WASP service. Jean says, "B.J. was a most remarkable woman. As a Commanding Officer she was outstanding. She kept a 'tight ship' but did so with extreme fairness. You always knew what was expected of you. She had a wonderful personality – always upbeat, friendly, encouraging, helpful and with a happy positive outlook. B.J. was one of the best organizers I've ever known and she was younger than all of us. I learned a great deal from her. She is terribly missed by all of us who knew and loved her – Amazing Woman!" B.J. was born July 1, 1920 in Seattle Washington, and died at 93 on July 7, 2013 in Los Gatos, California.

B.J. Erickson was one of the 28 original WAFS under Nancy Harkness Love's Command. She learned to fly at 19 and in 1940, became the first woman to be recruited into the CPTP at Long Beach's Daugherty Field. She went through the entire four-part program and added many hours of flight time into her logbook. In September 1942, Nancy Love selected her to command the AAF ATC Ferrying Squadron at Daugherty Field in Long Beach, California. At 22, B.J. was commanding a

Squadron of women whose numbers eventually reached 100. Some women were ten years her senior. Among her wartime feats in the ATC was flying four 2,000-mile trips in five days. She was the only woman during the war to be awarded the Air Medal for her service. One of the WASP stories B.J. told was about a layover in Denver where she and three male pilots, all in uniform, tried to check into a hotel. The hotel refused to let B.J. register because no single woman was allowed to stay at the hotel. The male pilots stayed and she was taken to a sleazy motel in another part of the city.

After deactivation of the WASP in December of 1944, B.J. married Jack London. They had two daughters, Terry and Kristy, and both became pilots. Terry London Rinehart had three children, Kerry, Justin and Laura and all are pilots. B.J. and Jack London operated United States Aviation flight school until the Korean War. Her husband preceded her in death by 40 years and one day. She served as the first Chair of the Long Beach Chapter that created and managed the Powder Puff Derby, also called All-Woman Transcontinental Air Race (AWTAR). She flew in many of the races. For her WASP service, in 1948 B.J. received a commission as a Major in the U.S. Air Force Reserve. She would go on to found and operate Barney Frazier Aircraft, Inc., in Long Beach with her younger daughter, Kristy London Ardizzone. In 2006, a street near the airport was named "Barbara London Drive" in her honor. Barbara's legacy includes her role as an inspiration for women pilots. She figures prominently in the Long Beach Airport's history exhibits, along with other great Long Beach-based female pilots, including Gladys O'Donnell and Kay Daugherty.

14: *Jean's Later Years*

Profile of Virginia "Ginny" Hill Wood

Ginny Hill was a WASP 43-4 classmate of Jean's and they moved along parallel paths. Both learned to fly in the CPTP and were stationed at Daugherty Field in Long Beach. Both were selected to go to Instrument School in St. Joseph, Missouri; Pursuit/Fighter School in Brownsville, Texas; and Officer Candidate School in Orlando, Florida. They kept in touch and corresponded until Ginny died at 95 on March 8, 2013 at her home in Fairbanks, Alaska.

Ginny Hill was born October 24, 1917 in Moro, Oregon and grew up in rural Washington where she skied, hiked, went river rafting and guided horseback trips. She took her first plane ride at age 4 sitting in her father's lap as they flew with a barnstorming pilot. When she was 10, she followed the national news reports of Charles Lindbergh and Amelia Earhart, as Jean had done.

When WASP were deactivated, Ginny was one of the lucky ones to get flying jobs with good pay. She worked as a pilot transporting cargo, flying war-surplus planes to Alaska, and leading airline tourist trips. Ginny bicycled through Europe before WWII and again after the war in 1948 with her close friend Celia Hunter (WASP 43-5). Ginny said, "So the war was over and the youth of Europe was on the road. Going there changed our lives .... It made us citizens of the world."

Karen Brewster edited and published Wood's memoir *Boots, Bikes, and Bombers: Adventures of Alaska Conservationist Ginny Hill Wood*. (3) It is called a testament to the joys of living a life full of passion and adventure. Following are excerpts from that book. Ginny writes that women pilots

> . . . got six dollars per day per diem. The men got seven dollars. When we were off delivering planes and had to spend the night along the way, if you stayed on base, you could stay for one dollar and fifty cents a night in the barracks. If you went to town, it would cost you five dollars to stay in a hotel. That's what most girls did. They'd never been away from home and they thought boy, they wanted to live it up. They'd take a taxi, eat meals out, go to the bars and spend all their money. I'd stay in the barracks and eat in the enlisted men's mess for fifty cents, which I could do, instead of going to the officer's club which was more expensive and where you had to wear a dress. Nobody knew quite what we women were supposed to do, so we could go to either place. Not only did I save money by staying on post, but I could get up in the morning, get down to the airfield early to have the first ground crew start my plane, and I'd be at the next stop before those women who were in town got a taxi, came back to base, and waited for a ground crew to come and start their plane.

Ginny's favorite plane, like Jean's, was the P-51 Mustang. She says, "Everything in the cockpit was logical. If your gear went up, your toggle switch went up." She contrasted the P-51 with the P-40 and says "the switches and levers were spread out all over the cockpit so you're trying to find what you need next. You were doing gears over here, and gas over there. And if you wanted to make this gear go up, this switch would go down."
Ginny writes, "I think why I loved flying is because

I began to see the earth from another perspective. That always stayed with me. When I was ferrying planes, the one thing you were supposed to do was to stay over flat lands so if you had an emergency, there were fields you could land in. But I didn't do this. I went exploring, I can remember flying P-51s and P-38s that had never been in the air before and taking them over the Sierras and over the red rock country in New Mexico. I was always looking down to find places that I'd want to go hiking when the war was over. I did go back later and find some of those very places I had looked down at." (3)

In 1950 Ginny married Morton "Woody" Wood, a Forest Ranger. The Woods and Celia Hunter pooled their resources to buy land in the Alaska wilderness under the Homestead Act and in 1952 built Camp Denali as a tourist outpost and base for backcountry exploration. The Woods were married for ten years and had a daughter, Romany. Ginny and Celia continued to operate Camp Denali. Together they co-founded the Alaska Conservation Society in the late 1950s, and lobbied President Eisenhower to designate the Northeastern region of Alaska as a federally protected wilderness in 1960. The Arctic National Wildlife Refuge is the largest national wildlife refuge in the U.S.

"Ginny's philosophy and approach to life was cherishing nature and friends, fighting for what you believe in, living a simple life and not leaving a big footprint." Her column, "From the Woodpile," was published in the Northern Alaska Environmental Center's newsletter for twenty-three years. Wood guided her last backcountry trip at age 70, cross-country skied into her mid-80s and gardened into her early 90s.

Ginny received her Congressional Gold Medal from Alaska Senator Lisa Murkowski on April 2, 2010 at Fairbanks.

EPILOGUE

By 2016, 75 years after WWII began, the U.S. military finally allowed women to serve in all combat roles. Former Defense Secretary Ash Carter said,

> As long as they qualify and meet the standards, women will now be able to contribute to our mission in ways they could not before. They'll be allowed to drive tanks, fire mortars, and lead infantry soldiers into combat. They'll be able to serve as Army Rangers and Green Berets, Navy SEALS, Marine Corps Infantry, Air Force Parajumpers and everything else that was previously open only to men.

Former President Barack Obama called the move a "historic step forward," and said it would "make our military even stronger.

Ash Carter believes the U.S. can't build a "force of the future" by excluding half of the country's population. About 10 percent of military positions, or 220,000 jobs, were closed to women prior to 2016. In 2017, women are nearly 20% of recruits, 15% of the active duty and 18% of the reserves. More than 345,000 women have deployed since September 11, 2001. Female veterans are expected to top two million by 2020. Still, there is a long way to go for the general public to equally honor every woman and man who has worn a uniform and for the Veteran's Administration to replace their motto on plaques outside their offices across the country, "To care for him who shall have borne the battle and for his widow, and his orphan." A. Lincoln

Senator Jon Tester of Montana introduced The Deborah Sampson Act in March 2017 with 15 cosponsors, to change the Veteran's Administration culture and to honor women veterans. The Act addresses gender disparities at the VA and ensures that women veterans are getting equitable care. In September 2018, there are 13 more cosponsors for a total of 28, but the legislation remains stalled in the Committee on Veterans' Affairs. The Bill would expand care for newborn children of women veterans, require that every VA facility have at least one full- or part-time women's health primary care provider on staff, require a complete report on the availability of prosthetics for women veterans, initiate a peer-to-peer counseling pilot program for women veterans who are separating from the military and most at risk of becoming homeless, centralize all information for women veterans in one easily accessible location on their website and require that the VA motto be more inclusive.

May 16, 2017, Dr. Heather Wilson became the 24th Secretary of the Air Force over 660,000 active-duty, Guard, Reserve, and civilian forces with a budget of $132 million. Wilson earned a doctorate degree as a Rhodes Scholar at Oxford University in England in 1985. She was a 1982 graduate from the Air Force Academy in Colorado Springs. The prohibition on women flying combat aircraft until 1993 was part of the reason she did not pursue a career as a pilot again after earning her doctorate.

Out of Jean's WASP experience came lifelong friendships, an unshakeable confidence in herself and her ability, rock-solid self-sufficiency, and knowledge that she can tackle anything. Jean is proud that she served her country in wartime and would have gone into combat.

After WASP deactivation Jean chose a life of university teaching. She would have stayed with the WASP and the job she loved if Congress hadn't deactivated them. She has moved from a natural shyness to saying yes to speaking engagements and making the DVD "She Wore Silver Wings". Jean's value of self-sufficiency served her well when she split her time living half of each year in the peaceful solitude of rural Idaho and the other half in El Cajon, California. Even now she wants to fix things herself and only reluctantly calls a handyman.

Jean is grateful for her wartime experience, short-lived as it was. She says, "Every experience in life does change one. I would do it all over again in a heartbeat. Period."

APPENDICES

A: Profile of Nancy Harkness Love

Nancy Harkness was born February 14, 1914 in Houghton, Michigan, the daughter of a wealthy physician. At 16 she took her first flight and earned her pilot's license within a month. She attended Milton Academy in Massachusetts and Vassar in New York. At Vassar she earned extra money taking students for rides in an airplane she rented from a nearby airport. In 1936 she married Robert Love, an Army Air Corps Reserve Major. Nancy was a Pilot for their Inter City Aviation business in Boston, and also for the U.S. Bureau of Air Commerce. In 1937 and 1938 she was a test pilot including for the new three-wheeled landing gear. She helped mark water towers with town names as a navigational aid for pilots.

In 1942, Nancy's husband Robert Love was called to active duty in Washington, D.C. to serve as Deputy Chief of Staff of the Ferry Command. Nancy Love took a civilian post with the AAF Air Transport Command, Ferrying Division Operations Office in Baltimore, Maryland. She commuted daily in her own plane from their home in Washington, D.C.

Nine months after Pearl Harbor was attacked, General Arnold reversed his position and asked Love to find experienced female pilots to ferry planes in the U.S. He created the Women's Auxiliary Ferrying Squadron (WAFS) with Love as Commander. By September 1942, Nancy Love was Commander of the Women's Auxiliary Ferrying Squadron (WAFS), part of the AAF Air Transport Command. Among the 28 women she selected to serve were: B.J. Erickson, Betty Gillies, Cornelia Fort, and Evelyn Sharp.

B.J. Erickson said,

> Nancy was in the field flying the same airplanes we were flying ... where Jackie (Cochran) was sitting in an office (in Washington) administrating a large program, and it had to get larger and larger to make her bigger and bigger. Nancy was very well educated; she was a very talented administrator as far as working with people. We would've done anything in the world she said, because we knew her decisions were right. Plus the fact she asked our opinion. We had staff meetings. As a Squadron Commander I went back to Cincinnati at least two or three times a year for staff meetings so that we knew what we were supposed to be doing within the Squadron cause I had eighty girls in Long Beach that I was responsible for . . ." "I got along with Nancy very well .... We kept track of each other for a while. I became better friends with her Deputy, and Squadron Commander in Wilmington, Delaware, Betty Gillies.

Betty Huyler Gillies, another of the 28 WAFS originals, said in 1976,

> The success of the WASP program within the Ferrying Division was due largely to Nancy Love's ability to organize, to lead and to cooperate with the 'powers that be' within the Division. She had the respect of all with whom she worked, smoothly and efficiently

from its start in September 1942 until deactivation in late December 1944.

At the end of the war, Love and her husband were decorated simultaneously. He received the Distinguished Service Medal, and she the Air Medal for her "Operational leadership in the successful training and assignment of over 300 qualified women fliers in the flying of advanced military aircraft." In 1948 Nancy Harkness Love became a Lieutenant Colonel in the U.S. Air Force Reserve. Love died of cancer at 62 on October 22, 1976 at Martha's Vineyard, Massachusetts. She did not live to see the WASP receive military recognition one year later. After her death a box was found with her belongings that held photographs, newspaper clippings, and her handwritten list of the 38 women pilots that lost their lives flying in service to our country. Deanie Bishop Parrish (WASP 44-4), Associate Director of "Wings Across America" says, "Her job had not been easy, but the love and respect she received from the WAFS and WASP she commanded during WWII is indisputable."

APPENDICES

B: Profile of Jacqueline Cochran

Jacqueline Cochran was born Bessie Pittman on May 11, 1906 in Muskogee, Florida, the youngest of five children. Her father was an itinerant worker in saw mill camps. The Pittman's raised her from infancy and eventually told her they were not her real parents. She remained in contact with her foster parents and later contributed to the support of their children and grandchildren. Cochran worked from a very young age in a textile mill, then in her teens was hired by a beauty shop to sweep floors where she learned to cut hair. She married at 14 and had a son who died in 1925 when he was five years old and she was 19. She changed her name to Jacqueline Cochran, moved to New York and worked as a beautician in the Saks Fifth Avenue Hair Salon. She developed a line of cosmetics sold through Jacqueline Cochran, Incorporated and was a successful business woman.

In 1932, at a Miami dinner party, Cochran met the man who became her second husband, Floyd Bostwick Odlum. He suggested she learn to fly to market her beauty products and she earned her pilot license that same year when she was 26 years old. Odlum was a wealthy financier, President of Floyd Atlas Utilities and Investors Co. Ltd., 14 years her senior, and married with 3 children. In 1936 Odlum and Cochran married, and in 1938 Cochran began air racing and setting new transcontinental and international records. Cochran set many distance, speed and altitude records, and was the first woman to break the sound barrier in 1953.

After General Arnold turned down her proposal to

have experienced female pilots do domestic noncombat flying, she organized 25 U.S. female pilots to fly with the British Air Transport Auxiliary. She returned to the U.S. immediately after General Arnold announced the creation of the WAFS under the command of Nancy Love. Cochran lobbied him successfully for a Women's Flying Training Detachment (WFTD).

In 1945 Jackie Cochran worked at the Pentagon as a special consultant to General Hap Arnold and was awarded the Distinguished Service Medal and Distinguished Flying Cross for her wartime service. In 1948, she finally received her military commission, as Lieutenant Colonel in the U.S. Air Force Reserve. Cochran retired from the Reserve in 1970 as a Colonel.

Politically ambitious, Cochran ran for Congress in California's 29th District in 1956. She defeated the five Republican male opponents but lost to the Democrat and first Asian-American congressman Dalip Singh Saund. Saund won with 54,989 votes (51.5%) to Cochran's 51,690 votes (48.5%). Her political setback was one of the few failures she ever experienced and she never attempted another run. Those who knew Cochran have said that the loss bothered her for the rest of her life.

In 1970 Cochran developed heart problems and received a pacemaker. After that she retired from flying to her home in Indio where she enjoyed: traveling, bike riding and working in her vegetable garden. Her husband died in 1976 and the following year, the WASP finally received the promised militarization. She died August 9, 1980 at 74 in Indio, California.

APPENDICES

C: WWII Female Pilots in England

Britain's Air Transport Auxiliary (ATA) was a British civilian organization that was active during WWII, from February 15, 1940 to November 1945. They were based at White Waltham Airfield in Berkshire, England. The initial plan was that the ATA would carry mail and medical supplies, but the pilots were immediately needed to work with the Royal Air Force (RAF) Ferry Pools transporting aircraft. By May 1, 1940 the ATA had taken over transporting all military aircraft from factories to Maintenance Units to have guns and accessories installed. On August 1, 1941 the ATA took over all ferrying jobs to free the much-needed pilots for combat duty.

The ATA recruited pilots who did not qualify for the Royal Air Force because of age or fitness. They were humorously referred to as "Ancient and Tattered Airmen". The ATA had 168 women pilots (about 12%) and they were paid the same as male pilots. In September 1942 Jacqueline Cochran and 25 women pilots from the U.S. volunteered to serve with the ATA. Other women volunteered from Britain, Canada, Australia, New Zealand, South Africa, Poland, Argentina, Chile and the Netherlands. They flew 38 types of aircraft without radios, relying on compasses and Bradshaw's Railway Guides. Fifteen women lost their lives flying with the ATA.

D: Jean's WFTD Acceptance Letter from Army Air Force, Flying Training Command

ADDRESS REPLY TO
COMMANDING GENERAL
AAF. FLYING TRAINING COMMAND
TEXAS AND PACIFIC RAILWAY BLDG.
FORT WORTH, TEXAS

ARMY AIR FORCES

HEADQUARTERS FLYING TRAINING COMMAND

FORT WORTH, TEXAS

201- Landis, Jean

29G

JAN 1 2 1943

Miss Jean Landis
2448 F. Street
San Diego, California

Dear Miss Landis:

Your application for admission to the Women's
Flying Training program has received favorable consideration.

It is desired that you report at your own expense
at 10:00 A. M., March 15, 1943, to the Commanding Officer,
Woman's Flying Training Detachment, Municipal Airport, Houston,
Texas. Sufficient allowance should be made for possible delays
as transportation difficulties will not be accepted as an
excuse for late arrival. Upon arrival at Houston, report by
telephone for further instructions.

You should bring with you this letter, identification
credentials, current CAA pilot license and your logbook.

Provisions have been made for your employment on
Civil Service status at the rate of $150 per month during
your satisfactory pursuance of flying instruction under Army
control. Upon satisfactory completion of the Army instruction
course, and if physically qualified, you will be eligible for
employment as a utility pilot at a rate of $250 per month,
subject to your satisfactory performance of the duties assigned
you.

No provision is made for your subsistence and maintenance during the term of this appointment. No uniform will
be issued during the period of the training course.

Please acknowledge receipt of these instructions
and your intention to report as directed.

For the Commanding General

Allen B. Black

ALLEN B. BLACK
Major, A.G.D.
Assistant Adjutant General

APPENDICES

E: Jean's Letter from War Department, Army Air Force at Large

Form AC-CP50

CHANGES IN CIVILIAN PERSONNEL
WAR DEPARTMENT
ARMY AIR FORCES AT LARGE
319th AAFFTD,
Municipal Airport, Houston
(Headquarters) Texas

1. Name   LANDIS, Jean   February 24, 1943
(Date)

2. Nature of Action   W.S.A. Reg V (Indef)

3. Effective Date   February 16, 1943

9 Report No.
Regular

10 Civil Service or other legal authority
Ltr. USCSC ro OSW
9-24-42

11 Appropriation
Regular

	From	To	
4. Position		Civ. Student Pilot (Uncl)	12 Date of Birth 9-28-18
5. Salary		$1800 per annum	13 Legal Residence Texas
6. Org'n Unit		AAF at large	14 Subject to Retirement Act? Yes
7. Headquarters		319th AAFFTD, Municipal Airport, Houston, Texas	
8. Dept'l or Field	FIELD	FIELD	15 Oath Taken 2-16-43

16. Remarks New Position   AAFPTC
Bureau Auth: Ltr. Hq. AAF to Commanding General, AAFGCTC, FortWorth, Texas 10-7-42, Subject: "Flying Training For Women".

"Under authority delegated by the Secretary of War in Orders M. dated August 13, 1942, and the directive, Commanding General, Army Air Forces, dated August 27, 1942 subject: Delegation of Authority and Responsibility for Civilian Personnel Actions in Field Activities."

18. Civil Service Authority   Under authority delegated by the Secretary of War in Orders No. dated December 23, 1941, and the directive of the Chief of the Air Corps dated January 7, 1942 you are notified of the above action concerning your employment.

17. Commanding Officer
A. R. MATHENY,
2nd Lt., Air Corps
Civ. Per. Officer.

W-6599,AC

89

F: WWII Female Pilots in Russia

During WWII, 800,000 women served in the Soviet Armed Forces. Russia's famous female pilot Marina Raskova personally lobbied Stalin to let her recruit and train three all-women squadrons of aviators, ground crews and mechanics. He authorized this on October 8, 1941 and the first unit flew into action in April, 1942. Raskova commanded a second unit, the Guards Bomber Aviation Regiment, until she was killed in a flying accident in 1943 at the age of 30.

The most famous of the three female squadrons was the 46th Taman Guards Night Bomber Aviation Regiment. In four years, the unit flew 30,000 missions and dropped 23,000 tons of bombs on the German invaders. If hit by tracer bullets, their mainly plywood and canvas planes would burn like sheets of paper. Each night, the 40 or so two-woman crews flew 8 or more missions, sometimes as many as 18.

Their obsolete single-engine Polikarpov Po-2 bi-plane crop-duster/trainers were so slow that pilots in Germany's frontline interceptors had trouble shooting them down. The Russian plane's top speed was well below the stall speed of the German planes. The pilots in the Luftwaffe fighters risked crashing if they tried to ease back on the throttle enough to engage the Soviet bombers. The bi-planes also had excellent gliding characteristics that allowed the pilots to kill their noisy engines as they approached a target and silently surprised the enemy. The attack technique of the night bombers was to idle the engine near the target and glide to the bomb release point with only a whooshing wind noise of the plywood and canvas wings to reveal their location. German soldiers likened the sound to broomsticks and named the pilots "Night Witches". The two women crews flew only at night with no parachutes, guns, or radios, only maps and compasses. By war's end, the squadron lost 30 pilots and produced 23 Heroes of the Soviet Union.

Nadeshda "Nadia" Popova was one of the first female military pilots and flew 852 missions. She died in 2013 at 91. Popova said, "Almost every time we had to sail through a wall of enemy fire." She was inspired both by patriotism and a desire for revenge as her brother was killed shortly after the Germans swept into the Soviet Union in June 1941. The Nazis had commandeered their home to use as a Gestapo police station. She was named Hero of the Soviet Union, the nation's highest honor. She was also awarded the Gold Star, the Order of Lenin and the Order of the Red Star.

APPENDICES

G: Excerpts from WASP "Final Report"
by Jacqueline Cochran

WASP (Women's Airforce Service Pilots), and before them the WAFS (Women's Auxiliary Ferrying Squadron) served our country during WWII from 1942 through 1944. They flew 60 million miles of Operations Flights with 9 million miles flown in Ferrying Operations. They flew 77 types of aircraft in 12,000 Ferrying Operations. Their flying duties included:

Ferrying
Towing targets for anti-aircraft
Engineering test
Towing targets for aerial gunnery
Demonstration
Tracking and searchlight missions
Check pilot
Simulated strafing and gassing
Administrative
Smoke laying and chemical missions
Flight Instructor (Basic and Instrument)

From the start, the training of women pilots covered:

1. Military Training: military courtesy and customs, Articles of War, safeguarding of military information, drill and ceremonies, Army orientation, organization, military corres-pondence, chemical warfare and personal affairs.

2. Ground School: mathematics, physics, maps and charts, navigation, principles of flight, engines and propellers, weather, code, instrument flying,

communications, and physical and first aid training.

3. Flight Training: primary through advanced training, which placed the graduate in line to take up operational duties immediately in all lighter type planes and to handle the faster heavier types after the usual short period of transitional training.

WASP training began in November 1942 for three months at the Municipal Airport at Houston, Texas with inadequate facilities and equipment. The flying equipment was obtained from surplus or obsolete stock at various fields and consisted of civilian aircraft with rarely two planes of the same type, which presented burdensome maintenance and training problems.

Early in 1943 the AAF Flying Training Command inactivated Avenger Field at Sweetwater, Texas, as a base for training Male Cadets, and made it available for the women's pilot training program. The first class entered at Avenger Field 21 February 1943, while part of the cadets were still there. By May 1943, the last class of cadets had graduated and the remaining women then at Houston were transferred to Sweetwater. The flying equipment at Avenger Field consisted of something over 200 airplanes of standard types, including PT-17's, PT-19's, BT-13's, BT-15's, AT-6's, AT-17's, UC-78's, UC-43's, and UC-81's.

At the start, the total program occupied 23 weeks from entry into training to graduation and assignment to a using agency of the Army Air Forces (AAF). During these 23 weeks the trainees had 115 hours of flying and 180 hours of ground school. At the end of the program the training period had been lengthened to 30 weeks, with 210 hours of Flight and 393 hours of Ground School, and a system of two-phase Flight Training (Primary and Advanced). Training took place at Avenger Field in Sweetwater, Texas and was the only AAF school where all phases of training were conducted at a single base. Later, more time was given to cross country flights.

The women pilots on Civil Service status could not exactly fit into the scale of pay of Army Air Forces military personnel. Trainees were paid $150 per month and with regulation over-time established by the AAF, received actually $172.50 per month. They had to pay their own transportation to Sweetwater and their way home in case of severance from the program prior to graduation. While at Sweetwater they paid $1.65 per day for maintenance.

After assignment to operational duties the women pilots received $250 per month which, with regulation overtime, brought the pay to $287.50 per month. While on their bases they paid $15.00 to $20.00 per month for quarters and had the privilege of buying their meals in the Officers' Mess. Both trainees and graduates customarily received the regulation allowance of $6.00 per day when away from base on official duty. The pay of a WASP on operational duty was slightly less than that of a 2nd Lieutenant with flight pay. There was no promotion or advancement in pay depending on length of service. All WASP and new graduates received the same pay.

At the conclusion of the WASP program in 1944,

the number of WASP on operational duty and flying status with the various air forces and commands were as follows:

Headquarters AAF	1
Training Command	620
Air Transport Command	141
First Air Force	16
Second Air Force	83
Fourth Air Force	80
Weather Wing	37
Proving Ground	11
Air Technical Service	6
Troop Carrier	3
Total	916

There were 38 WASP who died flying military planes during the war, and they received no military recognition. The army didn't pay for their burial expenses because the women were considered civilians. (2)

GLOSSARY

AAC	Army Air Corps
AAF	Army Air Force
AT	Advanced Trainer
ATC	Air Traffic Control
ATC	Air Transport Command
ATA	Air Transport Auxiliary
AWTAR	All Woman Transcontinental Air Race (Powder Puff Derby)
BT	Bomber Trainer
CAA	Civil Aeronautics Administration
CPTP	Civilian Pilot Training Program
FTC	Flying Training Command
OCS	Officer Candidate School
PT	Primary Trainer
RPM	Revolutions per minute
SPARS	Coast Guard Women's Reserve – contraction of their motto "Semper Paratus—Always Ready"
UC	Utility Aircraft
WAAC	Women's Auxiliary Army Corps
WAC	Women's Army Corps, previously known as WAAC
WAFS	Women's Auxiliary Ferrying Squadron
WASP	Women Airforce Service Pilots
WAVES	Women Accepted for Volunteer Emergency Services (Navy)
WFTD	Women's Flying Training Detachment

BIBLIOGRAPHY

1. "She Wore Silver Wings," DVD, Written and Directed by Devin Scott (Jean's Grand Nephew) and Produced by Jeanne Scott (2010; San Diego, CA: American Dream Cinema). This documentary short tells the story of Jean Landis, WASP and one of the unsung heroes of WWII, and the story of other "brave women who sacrificed everything to fly for the Army, but were quietly and unceremoniously disbanded when their country needed them the most." http:// www.americandreamcinema.com

2. Eisenhower Archives https://www.eisenhower.archives.gov

3. Brewster, Karen, Editor, *Boots, Bikes, and Bombers: Adventures of Alaska Conservationist Ginny Hill Wood (Oral History),* 2012, Fairbanks, University of Alaska Press

OTHER IMPORTANT WASP RESOURCES

"Female WWII Pilots: The Original Fly Girls," NPR, Susan Stamberg, March 9, 2010. http://www.npr.org/2010/03/09/123773525/female-wwii-pilots-the-original-fly-girls

Find a Grave: The 38 WWII WASP who died in service to their country. https://www.findagrave.com/

National WASP World War II Museum at Avenger Field, Sweetwater, Texas http://waspmuseum.org

Texas Woman's University, The Official WASP Archives http://www.twu.edu/library/wasp.asp

WASP Remembered by Those who Knew Them http://wwii-women-pilots.org Wings Across America is the WASP Site of WASP Deanie Bishop Parrish and her daughter, Nancy Parrish. There is extensive WASP information including: WASP Timelines, Photos from then and since, Information about the 38 who died, and much more. www.wingsacrossamerica.org

Women of Courage 2010 – WASP History, Biographies and more http://sandpoint.org/womenofcourage/

Women's Home Companion July 43 "At the twilight's last gleaming" by Cornelia Fort http://www.wingsacrossamerica.us/records_all/wasp_articles/twilight.pdf

Made in the USA
Middletown, DE
24 September 2019